THE YORKSHIRE DALES

Biographies and Acknowledgements

Photographs by E. A. Bowness, Norman Duerden & David Tarn

Ted Bowness was born into an old Cumbrian family and now lives in a South Lakeland
village. He sold his first photograph to *Motorcycle Magazine* and later established his own picture library, specialising in Cumbria and the Yorkshire Dales. In 1978 he produced
a book of his photographs which sold over 100,000 copies.

To Maureen of the Eagle Eye
Naturalist, artist and writer **Norman Duerden** took his first nature pictures with an ancient
hand-and-stand plate camera. Two decades later he began a long series of wildlife colour
studies; these have been used by the BBC and as illustrations for his many books on
Scotland, the Dales and natural history. A former College Vice Principal and Fellow
of the Royal Society of Arts, he now lives in retirement in the Ribble Valley.

For Christine, my long-suffering wife, and for Dominic and Sara
David Tarn lives with his young family in North-East England, within easy access
of the Yorkshire Dales and other areas of scenic beauty. He is a self-taught photographer
who turned his hobby into a career in 1993. He now runs his own picture library and under-
takes photographic commissions.

Text by Anna Newland

For Vic
Anna Newland has lived near London all her life, but takes every opportunity to escape to
the Yorkshire Dales to indulge her hobbies of walking, painting and photography.

With grateful thanks to Fiona Rosher, Debbie Allen,
Denny Minnit, Sue Wood and Dave Jones.

Picture Credits
E.A. Bowness pp. 25, 31, 35, 36, 45, 51, 56, 59, 62, 65, 68, 73, 77, 94, 100, 104, 109, 112,
115, 116, 117, 120, 124, 125, 129, 132, 133, 134, 135, 136, 137, 138 (© **English Life
Publications Ltd**), 139, 141, 144, 145, 146, 147, 148, 149, 152, 154, 156, 157, 158, 160,
161, 163, 164, 167, 172, 178, 180, 181, 183, 186, 195. **Norman Duerden** pp. 18, 20, 21,
22, 23, 26, 27, 37, 40, 57, 78, 86, 91, 92, 95, 96, 97, 106, 108, 114, 128, 130, 131, 140, 171,
173, 185, 187, 189, 193. **Tim Grevatt** p. 165. **Anna Newland** pp. 39, 50, 52, 53, 81, 121,
179. **Peter W. Robinson** pp. 113, 127, 159. **David Tarn** pp. 14, 15, 17, 19, 24, 30, 33, 34,
38, 41, 43, 44, 46, 47, 49, 58, 61, 63, 64, 67, 69, 72, 75, 76, 79, 80, 83, 87, 89, 90, 93, 99,
101, 105, 107, 119, 142, 153, 162, 170, 175, 176, 177, 182, 188, 190, 191, 192.
The Bridgeman Art Library p. 197.

ISBN 0 75257 488 4

This is a Parragon Book
This edition published in 2002
Parragon
Queen Street House
4 Queen Street
Bath, BA1 1HE, UK

Copyright 1999 © Parragon

Produced for Parragon by Foundry Design and Production.
Printed in China

THE YORKSHIRE DALES

PHOTOGRAPHS BY
E. A. BOWNESS, NORMAN DUERDEN, DAVID TARN

 NORMAN DUERDEN   Ed Bowness

Text by Anna Newland

Contents

Contents by Region

Introduction

The curlew calls and the wind sighs, high up where the wild and lonely moors meet the sky. Here, five of the main rivers of the Yorkshire Dales have their beginnings, sweeping down from the high watershed of the Central Pennines to flow through some of the most wonderful countryside in England.

The rivers Ribble, Swale, Wharfe and Aire lend their names to the best known dales, each of them with its own distinct character; the river Ure runs through Wensleydale. They all cut through the thick white mass of rock, known as the Great Scar Limestone, which makes up the bones and some of the most outstanding features of the Dales landscape. Formed millions of years ago by a tremendous agglomeration of the bodies of the small creatures who swam and died in their warm tropical sea, it still displays their fossilised shapes.

Softer shales and sandstones, more subject to erosion, were later deposited, building up layers interspersed with the limestone over a long expanse of time. These layers were eventually topped by a thick, dark layer of 'Millstone Grit' – so called because of its widespread use for millstones.

A dramatic climatic change brought the ice sheets and the grinding glaciers which inched their way inexorably through the valleys, smoothing away any jutting spurs and carving the wide 'U'-shaped dales which we see today. With the ending of the last Ice Age, the glaciers retreated, leaving smooth hillsides and flat valley floors, and depositing the erratics, moraines and drumlins which are a feature of any glaciated landscape. Water pouring through the dales wrought its own changes, dissolving the softer rocks at a faster rate than the hard limestone, creating shelves and terraces, caves and pot-holes.

This is the remarkable landscape that nature has fashioned, although man too has shaped and marked this land. Life must have been harsh here, and Neolithic people were reluctant to venture far into the desolate uplands. They sheltered in southern caves, leaving the remains of bears and of the reindeer who would have grazed the mosses and grasses which had appeared on the sub-arctic, tundra-like landscape, so much different

from that of today. Later, grassland and trees colonised the area to create the more familiar scene which now exists.

The remains of some of the early people to settle here date from the Bronze Age. A trading people who laid crude field boundaries and marked out the first of the many paths and tracks which traverse this land. Then the advent of the Celts from the west ushered in the Iron Age, and plentiful evidence of their culture and settlements can still be identified in many parts.

The Romans also came to Yorkshire, bequeathing their long straight roads, and Anglian settlers introduced place names still used today in the southern Dales, where they found a rich soil, well-suited to their arable farming needs. The Danes came marauding – and then settled, leaving a legacy of Norse names in the villages of the higher ground further north.

The last wave of incomers came after 1066. The Norman tyranny was fiercely opposed but eventually enforced, and the invaders set about taking over land and forest for hunting, and building great castles such as Richmond and

Bolton. Under the Normans, the power of the monasteries and abbeys grew, and theirs was undoubtedly the greatest influence in the Dales.

Monks of the Cistercian order first settled here in the 12th century. Quick to recognise the value of the wool trade they ruthlessly took over vast tracts of land on which to graze their enormous numbers of sheep. With this repression and dispossession of the poor, the monks came to be feared and hated; indeed there are some who assert

that Robin Hood championed the poor here, from a base in Barnsdale forest, rather than from Sherwood.

The grip of the Monasteries lasted for 400 years, ending abruptly and devastatingly with Henry VIII's Dissolution. Social change came to the Dales with new landowners and merchants who prospered from the wool and cloth produced here, and from the extensive lead mines. They built the mills, a number of fine houses, and many cottages to house the rising population of miners and mill workers.

At the end of the 18th century, a new kind of invader came: the first tourists were inspired by the awakening national interest in the natural world. The middle classes arrived with the leisure to come and marvel at the richness and beauty of the lovely Dales, with their romantic ruins, mellow stone cottages and breathtaking scenery.

Artists and poets also came: Edwin Landseer sought inspiration for his romantic pictures, as did Thomas Girtin. Turner also painted here, delighting in the wonderful light so appropriate for his style of art. William and Dorothy Wordsworth were irresistibly drawn from their beloved Lake District, so close to the Dales; Charles Kingsley

also came to walk and to fish in the tarns, and it was here that he found the literary inspiration for his 'water babies'. The music of the Yorkshire-born composer Delius was inspired by the solitude and wildness of the high places; other musicians have been similarly affected by this area.

The Dales themselves produced the pioneering geologist, Adam Sedgewick, and the Kearton brothers, Cherry and Richard, who were among the first to promote the

Victorian enthusiasm for natural history. They went to great lengths to obtain what were, at that time, unique and amazing photographs.

By the turn of this century the Yorkshire Dales had become a great focus of interest for the more adventurous: the walkers, climbers and potholers. The Yorkshire Ramblers' club had also been formed and had managed to climb all of the Three Peaks – Ingleborough, Penyghent and Whernside – in ten and a half hours, and the Frenchman E. A. Martel had made the first descent into the pot-hole Gaping Gill.

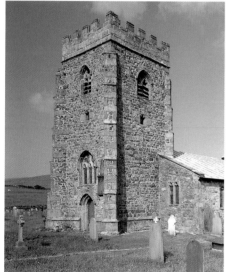

In 1954, 680 square miles of mainly privately owned land in the Yorkshire Dales were designated a National Park, and visitors came, encouraged by the veterinary surgeon and author Alf Wight, better known as James Herriott. His books and televised stories made the Yorkshire Dales familiar to people worldwide. J. B. Priestley and Howard Spring set novels here and film-makers frequently come, anxious to use the dramatic scenery as a backdrop.

However, this unique and beautiful landscape does not suffer from the surfeit of tourists that can afflict the Lake District and the West Country. Even in high summer, one does not have to venture far to enjoy pleasant riverside walks by meadows thick with wildflowers, cool rushing waterfalls and the wonderful aerial vistas, all in perfect solitude.

This magical scenery is set in a farming landscape, which belongs to the descendants of the tough and resilient people who have settled here throughout the centuries. As they go about their daily work, these no-nonsense Dalesmen and -women are always ready to offer a friendly welcome to the jaded urban dwellers who come to experience the magic and mystery of the glorious Yorkshire Dales.

THE DALES

Each of the renowned main dales of this area has its own particular character, but there are many lesser-known side dales and valleys whose quiet charm delights all those who discover them.

Swaledale Barns and Walls
NEAR GUNNERSIDE

The River Swale, the most northerly of the Dales rivers, meanders swiftly through a fertile valley which displays so many of the features that are the magic of the Yorkshire Dales. From the tiny cluster of cottages at Keld, with its waterfalls, to the elegant town of Richmond this rugged dale is a joy.

Ancient tracks run across the land, and miles of dry stone walls thread their way up the steep hillsides, dotted with many stone barns. Flanking the sinuous curves of the river, lush hay meadows flourish, for this is a pastoral landscape, and the hay provides winter feed for the animals, including the hardy, black-faced Swaledale sheep.

Pretty villages are strung out along the dale, and once housed the families of the miners during the height of lead production when, it is said, Swaledale lead was used for the roof of the Vatican.

As the river flows eastwards, the villages begin to take on a more prosperous aspect, and Bede's 'Rushing River' swirls triumphantly below the elegance and sophistication of Richmond, and on into the Vale of York.

Walden Valley
BISHOPDALE

The Walden valley is one of the 'secret' dales, for it is a side dale of Bishopdale, itself one of Wensleydale's larger tributary valleys.

At its lower end, where Walden Beck tumbles over small waterfalls, is the lovely village of West Burton, and at its head the road forks to run up either side of the stream. However, both of these roads end abruptly on the moorland and the valley runs up to Walden Head below towering Buckden Pike. It is this 'cul-de-sac' feature and lack of a through road which has ensured the preservation of the quiet and timeless air of this lovely valley.

Woodland flanks the stream and there is hardly any human intrusion, only the sheep which dot the hillsides and moorland, and on the lower pastures the cows grazing placidly.

This is an idyllic scene which has hardly changed for generations, and is one of the greatest delights of the Dales.

Langstrothdale Chase from Hubberholme
UPPER WHARFEDALE

Above the village of Hubberholme there is an extensive platform of limestone pavements which gives an unsurpassed view up the length of Wharfedale, showing the characteristic 'U'-shaped glacial valley, and to the right of this vantage point, a long, heavily wooded dale can be seen.

Langstrothdale is a beautiful and unfrequented tributary valley, which joins Wharfedale just to the north of Buckden, and the Chase was once a hunting preserve of the Norman Lords of Skipton. Fountains Abbey once owned the dale and its many outlying granges here, where their flocks of sheep were tended. On Cam Moor above this remote valley, the rivers Wharfe and Ribble are born, and the road which runs through Langstrothdale Chase becomes the moorland track of the Pennine Way. On Fleet Moss Moor, the herring-bone pattern of open ditches can be seen, and at the upper end of the dale, new conifer plantations are growing on pastures where the first experiments with lime and its benefit to crops were carried out in 1774.

Woodland
WHARFEDALE

The River Wharfe rises in the Askrigg block on Cam Fell, and at its small beginnings as a mountain stream it scampers down pretty little gills or ravines, and by limestone pavements and caves. The tributary valleys of Littondale and Langstrothdale add their own magic to Wharfedale and its bewitching and varied landscape.

The wild and lonely moors roll out above this broad glaciated valley, with its luxuriant meadows and pretty villages strung out along the river. From its source the Wharfe is always fast moving, its meandering passage is deceptive and it can be treacherous. At one stage, it hurls itself through a narrow wooded ravine with such fury that it changes its name. Here, where many have lost their lives, it is known as the Strid.

The river is subject to sudden rises in its levels and the bridges which span it are strongly fortified for they replace many others which have been swept away by the river in spate.

Evening
LITTONDALE

The setting sun casts a glow over one of the lovely tributary valleys of Wharfedale. Littondale has seen much of the history of the Yorkshire Dales and shadows cast by the lowering sun bring the medieval farming terraces, or lynchets into sharp relief on the slopes. The Norman aristocracy hunted here, and old tracks lead on to Settle and cross the high ridge into Wharfedale. Litton village, which gives its name to the dale, is situated in the shadow of Darnbrook Fell, to the eastern side of Fountains Fell, where shallow depressions indicate that coal was once mined here.

Littondale's best known village is Arncliffe. Surrounded by sloping moorland it is situated on a well-drained bed of gravel, which raises it above the dampness of the flat valley floor, its limewashed houses surrounding a pretty green. Charles Kingsley stayed here and Littondale was the model for Vendale in his story of *The Water Babies*.

Beside the River Skirfare stands the church of St Oswald's where the names of Littondale men who fought at the Battle of Flodden Field in 1513 can be seen – names still found in the dale today.

Sunset
RIBBLESDALE

The River Ribble is the only main dale river to run westwards from the Pennine watershed, and its dale is also exceptional for its geology. Ribblesdale displays all the extraordinary features of typical karst scenery, where sudden underground drainage occurs in a limestone landscape. This results in dry valleys, caves, pot-holes and sink holes, and the biggest and most impressive in the country can be found along the Ribble's course.

Where Fell Beck drains into Ingleborough's Gaping Gill, it disappears to plunge 340 feet. This famous pot-hole is reputed to be spacious enough to hold York Minster. Hull Pot on Penyghent is another mighty chasm where heavy rainfall causes a cascade of water which is swallowed up and disappears.

In Ribblesdale these vanishing watercourses eventually surface again from many famous caves which are often long distances from the swallow holes. The water tumbling into Gaping Gill flows out at the capacious White Scar Cave, which is a great attraction in itself, for its roof is hung with a mesmerising number of stalactites.

After it has rolled through this memorable landscape the Ribble continues its westerly journey; it is the only Dales river to flow into the Irish sea.

Great Coume
DENTDALE

On the slopes of Great Coume to the south of Dent village, wildflowers grow in glorious profusion, just one of the splendours of this very beautiful dale. Gentle green slopes rise on either side of the River Dee, feeding it with a host of small streams and becks that drain their heights. The valley is dotted with whitewashed farmhouses and the stone walls which lace their way across the eastern dales are replaced here by trees and hedgerows.

There are signs of quarrying in Dentdale as the Victorian penchant for everything black, and the fashionable interest in geology, led to the

great popularity of Dent marble. This is not really marble, just a very dark form of limestone, but it can be polished to an attractive gloss which reveals the white outline of its fossils. The quarrying of this highly prized rock became an important industry, and the Mill at Arten Gill was converted for the cutting of the limestone 'marble'. Unfortunately, the prosperity that this brought did not last, and the importing of cheaper Italian marble sounded the death knell of the industry which was finished by the end of the last century.

Woodland Scene
NIDDERDALE

Nidderdale is the shortest of the main dales and the river Nidd drains into the Ouse and the Humber estuary, as do the Swale, Ure, Wharfe and Aire.

Upper Nidderdale is a wonderful moorland wilderness, providing challenging and exhilarating country for serious walkers. There are two great reservoirs in this area and the utilitarian nature of these 'lakes', which provided Bradford's water, was part of the reason for Nidderdale's exclusion from the National Park. However, as part of the Corporation Waterworks the public were kept away from the reservoirs. Thus they have been preserved, as unspoiled as if they had been protected as conservation areas.

The Nidderdale Way runs from Scar House reservoir and past the village of Middlesmoor on its astonishing perch. High on a ridge, it has the dramatic landscape of the steep ravine of the Nidd on one side, and How Stean Gorge on the other. The Nidd sweeps on past pretty woodland, and Gouthwaite reservoir which has become an important waterfowl preserve.

Beyond the dale's market town of Pateley Bridge, the landscape becomes more commonplace, but as so much of Nidderdale's scenery can equal the magnificence of the other Dales, one can only hope that the National Park's omission will be rectified.

Redshank
COVERDALE

In the quiet valley of Coverdale a redshank sits on her nest, well camouflaged by her plumage. These birds are waders and are generally found on open shoreland, where they feed on the small shellfish and lugworms of which they find plenty in the mud. They are year-round residents in this country and usually they gather in flocks, but during the breeding season pairs seek the seclusion of some damp corner, where they build a nest on the ground.

Coverdale has proved a favourite site, and the redshank is just one of the unusual birds which have discovered its peace and solitude. This tranquil and heavily wooded valley, Wensleydale's most southerly tributary valley, is a delight to discover. The River Cover joins the Ure at East Witton, and the unfrequented road that runs the length of the dale was an important packhorse trail, linking Wensleydale with Wharfedale at Kettlewell. The village of Horsehouse, halfway along the dale was the main resting place for travellers before the steep climb up on to the moors.

The Setting Sun
WENSLEYDALE

Wensleydale derives its name from its old capital town of Wensley, but the population there was decimated by the plague in the 16th century, and Hawes and Leyburn are now the dale's most important towns.

The wide water meadows of Wensleydale spread out below the woodland on its gently sloping hillsides. This pastoral scenery differs markedly from the other dales, for here is dairy country, and cows grazing the lush herbs and grasses have produced the milk for Wensleydale cheese for hundreds of years.

Down the ages, people came to this dale to settle and they all left their imprint: neolithic caves, ancient earthworks, Roman roads and a fort, and many Norse names. 'Abbotside' demonstrates the links with Jervaulx Abbey which once owned much of the land here.

The Pennine Way, and many other roads and paths converge here in this lovely dale which is literally awash with splendid waterfalls. The memorable scenery has long enticed our poets and artists; indeed, Turner returned again and again to capture on canvas the beauty of this wonderful, light-filled dale.

Farmhouse
GARSDALE

The landscape to the west of the high watershed near Garsdale Head, changes dramatically from that of Wensleydale to the east, with its wide valley and meadows. Garsdale is a deep, narrow trough, with much woodland, and the farms are spaced out along the lower valley sides.

This isolated farmhouse is one of a sprinkling of buildings, where the Viking names of the original settlements still remain. Dandra Garth and Thursgill are now the names of farms here. The only cluster of houses is to be found at Garsdale Head, close to the railway station (on the Settle to Carlisle line). It was once known as Hawes Junction, but the line to Hawes and along Wensleydale to Leyburn was closed in 1964.

Towards the end of Garsdale there is the Adam Sedgewick trail and the many waterfalls of the awesome Howgill Fells, a picnic area which provides unsurpassed views over the unenclosed moorland of Longstone Fell.

Ingleborough
FROM KINGSDALE

To the west of little-known Kingsdale, is the last visible presence of the great single bed of limestone which lies across Ingleborough, from Wharfedale to the east.

A terminal moraine of boulder clay was left when a glacier of the last ice-age melted, and a lake was formed in Kingsdale. Eventually, the waters breached the dam, and today Kingsdale Beck cascades over Thornton Force at the top of the Ingleton ravine.

This unfrequented dale, leads on to Dentdale in the north, and there are several footpaths across the lonely moorland. One of these is Turbary Road, where horse-drawn sleds used to transport peat cut from the moors, bringing it down to be used for fuel at Ingleton.

The spectacular caves of Ingleborough lie just to the east of Kingsdale, and sink-holes and caverns abound on this 'Last Frontier' of limestone, including Ease Gill. This is the largest cave system in Britain, and higher up the dale, hidden amongst the trees of little Yordas Wood, is Yordas Cave.

This was once a show cave but has been long forsaken, for it was prone to flooding. The steps still remain, and it is possible to glimpse the main chamber with its ribbon-like waterfall.

Butterflies at Beck House
MALHAM, AIREDALE

Malham Beck is one of the prettiest in the Dales, babbling from the foot of the cliff at Malham Cove, and past Beck House with its ancient clapper bridge.

Above the cove is Malham Tarn, a rare upland lake, whose waters are held in the limestone by a bed of non-porous slate. The water flows out of the lake and disappears into sink holes above the cove, and it is often assumed that the little beck's appearance, issuing from a narrow slit below, marks the resurgence. However, the outflow from the tarn does not reappear until a point south of the village, known as Aire head. The drama of Malham Cove and Gordale Scar is a complete contrast to the lush dairy pastures and pretty villages to the south

The Aire has a comparatively short run within the Yorkshire Dales, and from its beginnings to Gargrave, its dale is commonly known as Malhamdale. It has some wonderful walking country, and the Pennine Way footpath follows the river closely.

Gargrave is situated on the Aire Gap. Travellers and transport have used this ancient pass through the 'Backbone of England' since time immemorial and here the sparkling Aire sweeps southeast to Skipton and out of the Dales.

TOWNS & VILLAGES

Throughout the Dales, picturesque villages are legion. From whitewashed cottages to those built entirely of local stone, they blend with the glorious scenery, and the elegant larger towns retain the air of pleasant market towns.

Bainbridge
WENSLEYDALE

The houses and large green of Bainbridge are situated on both sides of what was once the main turnpike road running through Wensleydale. Most of the houses are about 200 years old, and at Low Mill corn milling took place until about 1920; after that time it became a dairy producing Wensleydale cheese. In 1947, during severe flooding, the river Bain burst through its dam and damaged the mill so severely that it could no longer be used. The Rose and Crown Inn was built in 1443, and in its hallway hangs the old curfew horn, which dates from the days when this community was a forest village.

Looking even further back in time, the Roman fort of Virosidium was built in AD 74 on the large drumlin which overlooks the village. It was perfectly situated on its hill which rises above the flat valley floor, overlooking both the Bain and the Ure. The road that the Romans built later became the turnpike road, and still runs on as straight as an arrow to Ingleton, continuing over Cam Fell as a track. Of the fort, only mounds and parts of the stone ramparts remain; a mere glimpse of how it looked when it housed a garrison of 500 men.

Malham Village
AIREDALE

This pretty village, with its limewashed cottages and outstandingly pretty beck, is host to all the visitors who come to marvel at the local limestone features of Malham Cove and Gordale Scar, and yet it remains utterly unspoilt.

Below its craggy geological formations, Malham village is set amongst Airedale's lush and gentle landscape of woods and pastures, where pleasant walks abound. The riverside path winds through flowery meadows, which hum with the sound of insects, and into Wedber Wood. Under its shady canopy is Janet's Foss, where water cascades over a large, green pillar of rock and tufa. Janet derives from the old name of Gennet, the name of a fairy queen who is thought to inhabit the cave behind the little waterfall, and certainly this pleasant little wood, where the young River Aire seems to whisper and chatter as it hurries over mossy rocks and pebbles, has all the qualities of a fairy dell.

Clapham Village
NEAR INGLEBOROUGH

The charming little village of Clapham is a rarity in the Dales, for it is full of trees. Tucked away in a thickly wooded valley, south east of Ingleborough, the cottages are built on either side of tree-lined Clapham Beck, and the village has no less than four bridges spanning its stream. Some of the picturesque waterfalls generate hydroelectric power for the grey stone houses, which are mostly 18th century. The church of St James is mainly Regency although it still retains its 12th-century tower.

Clapham is where the renowned Yorkshire Dalesman magazine has been published since 1939, although it has now been re-named The Dalesman. Another claim to fame is that Michael Faraday, the pioneer of modern electricity, was the son of the village Blacksmith.

Much of the village was owned by the Farrer family. Reginald Farrer was a distinguished botanist who became an authority on alpine flowers, and introduced very many new plants, earning him the title 'The Father of Rock Gardening'. There is some splendid walking country in the area, and Farrer has been commemorated with a nature trail leading through the private Ingleborough Estate with its lovely landscaped gardens, to the mouth of Ingleborough cave.

Thwaite
SWALEDALE

The cottages in the small village of Thwaite huddle together at the foot of Kisdon Hill, in the upper reaches of Swaledale. The pretty bridge and all the houses are built entirely of the local stone, blending harmoniously with the barns and walls which characterise this part of the dale.

Norsemen made their home in Thwaite, giving it a name which means 'clearing in a wood', suggesting that a forest probably flourished here before the land was cleared for farming. However, this isolated part of the dales was not settled to any great extent until a new wave of colonisers moved in, seeking suitable land for grazing their animals.

In the last century, this village was a lively place, for the men who mined the lead in Swaledale occupied the cottages. But then, in 1899 a tragic event occurred; a torrential flood swept down Thwaite Beck and engulfed the village, drowning almost every soul. The volume of water that poured through must have been enormous, for it is said that flowers uprooted from Thwaite were later found growing along the valley at the next village of Muker.

Sedbergh
GARSDALE

Sedbergh's church of St Andrew retains many original Norman features, although there are some 14th-century additions. It remains a venerable building, with old pews and alms boxes which add to the evocative atmosphere of centuries of history.

Nearby is the tiny marketplace where a market has been held since a charter was granted in 1251, but the old cross which once stood here was removed in 1897 and can now be found in the garden of the Quaker meeting house in Brigflatts. Some of the cobbled main street of Sedbergh has been designated a conservation area, and behind some splendid old houses are quaint alleyways and courtyards dating from Tudor times. There is also a 17th-century chimney breast, where Bonnie Prince Charlie is said to have hidden.

Sedbergh School was founded in 1525 by Roger Lupton and is now a famous public school. William Wordsworth sent his son John here, and Hartley Coleridge, the son of the poet, was a teacher here – until he was dismissed for drunkenness.

Burnsall
WHARFEDALE

Burnsall village lies in a glorious position on the River Wharfe. Its long bridge stretches gracefully from the grassy riverbanks and is sturdy enough to withstand the vagaries of the waters, which can rise alarmingly high. The bridge was bestowed in 1612 by William Craven who also endowed the grammar school (now a primary school). He was a local boy who made his fortune in London and became Lord Mayor from 1610 to 1612. On his return to the Dales he became a great benefactor.

The houses are all made of the local gritstone, a material usually reserved for lintels and cornerstones in the Dales. St Wilfred's church rises strikingly against the green hillside above the village and bridge. It has a Norman font and the churchyard contains some Anglo Norse gravestones. The Lychgate on the pretty village green is unusual as it is combined with the village stocks.

The lovely scenery makes this an ideal starting point for many long walks. One of the riverside paths leads to a little suspension bridge and a footpath to Hebden, providing access to the outstandingly beautiful surrounding countryside, with its woodland, moorland and pleasant pastures.

Dent Village
DENTDALE

Dent is a true picture-postcard village of whitewashed cottages, with dark sandstone roofs and twisting cobbled streets surrounded by verdant scenery. It also has the highest railway station in Britain, which stands at a height of 1,150 feet. Surprisingly, it is five miles from the village.

There is a granite fountain in the main street, placed here as a memorial to Adam Sedgewick, the local man who became a pioneer geologist, and the solid bulk of Saint Andrew's church can be seen rising above the village. It is a large building which was rebuilt in Victorian times, but it retains its Norman doorway and has a very attractive interior. The chancel floor is paved with shining Dent marble and there are some Jacobean box pews.

Dent was the hub of the hand-knitting industry – which once flourished in the Dales. People would come here to learn the craft, and women would gather to sing and knit in each others' homes; there were 'knitting galleries' in many of the houses. Today, there are still accomplished knitters here, as well as a thriving artistic community of craft workers, whose work is much sought after by the village's many tourists.

Halton Gill
LITTONDALE

Far up in the wilds of Upper Littondale, beyond the place where the beck-draining Penyghent meets the Skirfare, the tiny village of Halton Gill nestles into the undulating folds of the landscape. Viewed from the height of the Stainforth road the hamlet's isolation is starkly apparent, for the lonely moors roll away endlessly, entirely devoid of any other sign of habitation.

Most of Halton Gill's houses and farms, all of which cluster picturesquely around a small green, date back to the 17th century. In the days when the packhorse trails brought frequent travellers through this village it was a lively place, but now this is the most isolated village in the Dales.

Two miles higher up is the even lonelier farmhouse of Cosh House – the most remote single dwelling. Inaccessibility is an integral feature of this rugged countryside and frequently means loneliness and isolation. Often this has led to desolation and decay, as inhabitants of solitary farms and cottages have sought companionship in the more accessible areas, leaving the buildings to crumble away.

Whole villages have gone too and the only evidence of their existence, that still remains today, is the faintly discernible shapes in the land that they once occupied.

Grassington
WHARFEDALE

The pretty and quaint village of Grassington is, justifiably, a very popular tourist centre, yet it remains quite unspoilt. It retains all the charm of former, less hurried times, with Georgian houses and cottages surrounding its cobbled square, and lining its narrow sloping streets. Amongst the older cottages is the home of one Tom Lee who, in 1766, murdered the local doctor and threw the body into the Wharfe. Lee was hanged in York. The museum on the square has an absorbing display showing the history of farming and industry in Upper Wharfedale.

The discovery of lead on the nearby moors led to an increase in population and prosperity, and Grassington became a very lively place. This was tempered by John Wesley's visit here on his preaching tour (a plaque on 'Wesley's Barn' dated 1783 commemorates this trip). He had a sobering influence on the miners' notoriously wild ways, which had previously brought the village into disrepute.

Grassington today is a peaceful and pleasant place, surrounded by enchanting riverside walks, pretty waterfalls and cool woodlands.

Muker
SWALEDALE

Muker was originally a Norse settlement, but plentiful evidence of neolithic settlements has been discovered close to the village. It is the biggest of the unpretentious villages of Upper Swaledale, which lie strung out alongside the River Swale as it snakes along the valley.

The church stands high, set against the hillside, and has Elizabethan origins although Victorian embellishments and additions are more evident now. Built in 1580 it was a chapel of ease where coffin bearers would stop to rest before continuing their journey to the church at Grinton, and Queens Inn used to keep tankards especially for these coffin carriers.

There is a plaque in the church which commemorates Richard and Cherry Kearton who went to the school here and whose wildlife books and early photographs were received with such great acclaim. It was on Muker Moor that Richard met Sidney Galpin of Cassells publishing house, and the position he took up there provided the springboard for his distinguished career as a writer and lecturer.

Each September, the Muker Show takes place. Farmers and stockbreeders flock here, along with the general public, to see the animals being judged and to take part in the sporting events.

Kettlewell
WHARFEDALE

Evening descends on the tranquil village of Kettlewell and its bridge. The water flowing beneath the bridge bequeathed the town its Norse name, which means 'bubbling spring'. Kettlewell is the capital of Upper Wharfedale and grew in importance in the 13th century when it was given a market charter. Much of the land surrounding the village was once owned by Bolton Priory and the abbeys of Fountains and Coverham, and the many roads that led here are still to be seen. Later, the establishment of the important lead mining centre to the south of Kettlewell at Grassington, and the development of the local textile industry, led to most of the 17th- and 18th-century houses being built. The church was

added in Victorian times. There is a story that relates how one impoverished parson turned his house into an inn to supplement his income.

Kettlewell is situated in the most magnificent part of Wharfedale. Watched over by the bulk of Great Whernside and its limestone scars, the village lies quietly surrounded by Celtic fields and the picturesque lines of drystone walls which shoot up the green hillsides.

Hawes
WENSLEYDALE

When approaching Hawes along the Pennine Way, one's first view is of the pointed steeple of the Victorian church, followed by the rest of this bustling little town. St Margaret's church has a light and pleasant oak furnished interior, and was built in just one year (in 1850), at a cost of only £3,000.

The name 'Hawes' is derived from 'Hals' – a Norse word meaning 'neck' – indicative of the town's site between two ranges of hills. At 850 feet above sea level it is one of the highest market towns, and one of the most important in the Yorkshire Dales. Despite its popularity with tourists, Hawes exudes an old fashioned charm, with its busy weekly market, attractive houses and local craftsmen.

Perfectly situated in Upper Wensleydale there is easy access from the town to many rewarding walks, and a drive across Wether Fell and Fleet Moss Pass – at a height of 1,857 feet – offers truly breathtaking views.

With the coming of the railway in 1877, Hawes became established as the capital of Wensleydale, and in 1897 the cheese factory was opened. The rail link is gone, but the creamery continues to produce fine Wensleydale cheeses and draws crowds of visitors who come to see it being made.

Cottage in Thoralby
BISHOPDALE

One of Wensleydale's least known tributary valleys is Bishopdale, and Thoralby is one of its secret treasures. Hidden away from the Wharfedale road and close to Bishopdale Beck, it has an old mill and waterfall, and is set amidst delightfully varied scenery. Near the small village green is an ancient pinfold (an enclosure for cattle), and the houses which radiate away from it are mainly 18th century. The few modern houses blend in sympathetically. The old village paths lead to the other Bishopdale villages and into Aysgarth with its waterfalls.

The village commands a splendid view of Burton Moor and the high white gash of Dove Scar on the opposite side of the dale; grassy slopes rise up behind it leading to Thoralby moor. Cattle grazing in the meadows around Thoralby and flanking the beck, are an indication of its proximity to Wensleydale.

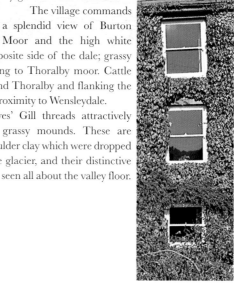

A walk through Thieves' Gill threads attractively through a scatter of large grassy mounds. These are drumlins; smooth lumps of boulder clay which were dropped and shaped by the Bishopdale glacier, and their distinctive 'basket of eggs' pattern can be seen all about the valley floor.

Cottages at Marske
SWALEDALE

Marske in Swaledale is a charming little village situated well away from the main road into Richmond, hidden amongst the farmland and richly wooded hills of a small tributary valley.

On a slope above Marske Beck, the little Norman church sits between the pretty rose-covered cottages of the village. St Edmund's dates from 1090 and still retains some of its original features, including the Norman door arches. This was once a forest village, and the valley was a Norman hunting chase – on the stone arch of the church's south doorway are the scratches and grooves where swords and arrows were sharpened.

There are later additions to this tiny church, dating from the 14th, 17th and 19th centuries. All the seating is in box pews which were put in by John Hutton of Marske Hall in 1823 – the pews reside respectfully over the graves of Hutton's father and grandfather. The church and its village have had close associations with Marske Hall ever since Matthew Hutton, the then Archbishop of York, acquired it in 1597. This graceful and well-proportioned house is situated amongst sloping lawns and ornamental gardens which spread up to the perimeter of the village.

Pateley Bridge
NIDDERDALE

Nidderdale does not lie within the Yorkshire Dales National Park area, but it is nevertheless one of the major dales. In contrast with other Dales villages, Pateley Bridge has a rather striking aspect, for its 18th- and 19th-century houses are built with the dark local gritstone. The medieval church was abandoned in 1827 for St Cuthbert's. When John Wesley came here on his tour of the north, the vicar allowed him to use the medieval church which was much larger than Wesley's preaching house. Wesley noted 'but it was not near large enough to contain our congregation'.

The village was granted a market charter in the 14th century and had an important position on the trading route from the Craven area to Fountains Abbey and Ripon. When steam replaced water power for the textile industry in the 19th century, the village's prosperity declined.

Pateley has also become renowned for its Folk Museum: an old Victorian warehouse housing a fascinating display in eleven rooms. It won the Natural Heritage Museum of the Year award in 1990.

Morris Men

REETH, SWALEDALE

Morris dancing is a ritual folk dancing tradition whose origins are uncertain but thought to derive from Moorish dance. The dancers are clad in white and wear bells. They often paint their faces, usually carry sticks and white handkerchiefs, and perform dances symbolic of various themes and rituals, many of which involve fertility.

These modern Morris Men are dancing on the large triangular green at Reeth, surrounded by its three-storey shops, and sprawl of 18th- and 19th-century houses and hotels. Reeth is much bigger than the other villages further up Swaledale, owing its more prosperous air to its lead mining history.

A huge weekly market used to be held here, when an amazing array of goods would be spread out on the green: clogs, ironmongery, meat and clothes were sold, and it was said that anything could be bought here 'from a pin to a pig'.

The Swaledale Folk Museum houses a fascinating and informative collection, showing the history of the dale – including lead mining, farming, village life and religion – and is very popular with the many visitors who flock here, also to stroll about the large, airy green and enjoy the wonderful wide view of the moors.

Leyburn
WENSLEYDALE

The name of Leyburn is derived from Le Borne, and is mentioned in the Domesday Book; this high market town is now the principal administrative centre for Wensleydale. It owes its importance to the de-population of nearby Wensley, during the plague of 1563, and to the Lords of Bolton Castle who ensured that the town received its market charter, albeit rather late, in 1684. Later, with the coming of the railway linking the town to Garsdale and the Settle to Carlisle line, Leyburn's continuing prosperity was ensured.

This is a very attractive town with inns, houses and shops surrounding a wide market place, where a busy weekly market is held. A short walk from the centre is Thornborough Hall, a large elegant building which houses the administration offices and the Tourist Information Centre. It was once the home of the Catholic Thornborough family, and the priest hole and secret cellars still exist as a reminder of the days when the performing of Catholic mass was forbidden.

Linton-in-Craven
WHARFEDALE

Linton-in-Craven is one of the most delightful villages in the Dales, apparently undisturbed by the passage of time. A small beck babbles below a sloping green, overlooked by the 17th- and 18th-century limestone houses and Fountaines Hospital. This row of six almshouses with its surprisingly impressive facade, was founded by Richard Fountaine. Born in Linton in 1639, he made his fortune in London, selling timber after the Great Fire. The hospital dominates the village with its grand Palladian style, and is generally ascribed to Sir John Vanbrugh, the architect of Castle Howard. Originally intended for poor men of the parish, it is still in use and now treats both men and women.

There is a Victorian bridge across Linton's beck, a 14th-century packhorse bridge, and an ancient clapper bridge. A ford and stepping stones ensure that the visitor has an abundance of ways to reach the little pub which nestles amongst the trees on the far side.

St Michael's is Linton's church, although it is some distance from the village. It stands picturesquely alone on the banks of the river Wharfe, and close to the tumbling waters of the shallow Linton Falls.

Settle
RIBBLESDALE

Beneath the towering crags of Warrendale Knotts and Attermire Scar, Settle is situated at the Aire Gap and is the gateway to the South Western Dales. It owed its importance initially to the traffic which came through here, and its further prosperity to the coming of the railway and the Settle to Carlisle line in 1876.

This very pleasant little town has consistently held a weekly market in its square for almost 750 years. On the market square stands a house with a plaque which proclaims that Elgar stayed here on his frequent visits to his friend Dr Buck, and on the site of the old open market is an arcade of shops, still known as The Shambles.

A Victorian fountain replaced the old market cross and it stands before an oddly named cafe; 'Ye Olde Naked Man'. This cafe was formerly an inn, and the name is a satirical comment on the elaborate fashions which once prevailed. The 'Old Naked Woman' can be found in Langcliffe.

Appropriately, the remains of the first settlers in the Yorkshire Dales have been found near Settle, in Victoria Cave, so named because it was discovered on Queen Victoria's Jubilee Day.

Mock Beggar Hall
APPLETREEWICK

Appletreewick is pronounced 'Aptrick' locally, and means 'dairy farm near apple tree'. This is a very pretty, one-street village, built on a slope which allows an unrestricted view of the magnificent countryside.

Despite being so small, Appletreewick has some notable houses dating from the 15th and 16th centuries. Low Hall is situated at the bottom of the street, and High Hall, at the top, was the home of William Craven, the great Dales benefactor. Having left his home town, he travelled by cart to London where he began his working life in a drapers shop – incredibly he went on to become Lord Mayor. When he returned, Craven restored the house which has three storeys and once had a two-storey porch.

The village was granted a market charter in 1311, raising it to the status of a town. This enabled the villagers to hold their 'Onion Fair.' The green track known as Onion Lane leads down to the banks of the Wharfe, where strings of onions were once sold.

Mock Beggar Hall, was once known as Monks' Hall. The village came under the ownership of Bolton Priory and this is the site of a monastic grange.

Old Courthouse
RIPON

Dwarfed by the glory of the cathedral's soaring west front, the old courthouse of Ripon shelters within a walled courtyard. In 886, the 'Liberty of Ripon' was granted by King Alfred the Great, this made Ripon independent of the West Riding of Yorkshire. The town's market charter was bestowed at around the same time. Because of this separate jurisdiction, the town required its own gaolhouse – in the 18th century, the old courthouse filled this post.

In 1836, when Ripon Minster became a Cathedral, Ripon became the smallest city in Yorkshire; however it still retains all the atmosphere of an old market town. This is a popular town with tourists, and the remarkable Law and Order Museums are a focus of great interest. The Prison and Police Museum in St Marygate provides us with a grim reminder of law enforcement in days gone by and there is a vast collection of police memorabilia including stocks, pillories and whipping posts.

The medieval town was centred around the cathedral and market square, but today the attractive houses are mainly Georgian and Victorian. The old Wakeman's house is a tenth century, half-timbered building, where the last Wakeman, Hugh Ripley lived. The Wakeman was the town's hornblower, and the custom of sounding the curfew at each corner of the square, every evening at nine o'clock, continues to this day.

WATERFALLS, RIVERS & LAKES

Everywhere within the Dales the sound of water is heard, splashing over rocks, rushing through narrow ravines or thundering into deep pools. Here can be found Britain's biggest falls and cataracts.

Hardraw Force
NEAR HAWES

At 96 feet Hardraw Force is the highest single drop cataract in England, and J.M.W. Turner came here to paint his Hardraw Falls, which shows the waterfall as an awesome torrent.

After heavy rainfall at its source on Abbotside Common, the Force is a spectacular sight, and the loud booming of the water as it drops into the pool below is strikingly amplified by the curve and overhanging rocks of this natural auditorium. During drier spells the water diminishes, and it is possible to walk behind the curtain of water where a recess has been carved out.

As well as beauty, Nature has also provided excellent acoustics and these have led to concerts being held here. For over one hundred years very popular annual brass band contests have also been held here.

Situated just a mile north of Hawes, the Force is reached via the Green Dragon Inn which exacts a small toll for access. An inn has been here for 750 years, although the toll bridge was probably the idea of an enterprising Victorian landlord. At that time, people would flock here to enjoy such spectacles as the famous acrobat Blondin, walking across the gorge on a tightrope. He even paused to fry some eggs when he was halfway across!

Upper Aysgarth Falls
WENSLEYDALE

The triple waterfalls at Aysgarth form a renowned beauty spot, and the very wide, shallow steps of the Upper Falls, make this one of the Yorkshire Dales' greatest attractions. People come to picnic in the waterside meadow and frolic in the many small cascades.

Middle Falls and Lower Falls drop more steeply through a narrower part of the limestone gorge below the bridge and the old Yore Mill. The mill was originally built in 1784 for spinning worsted yarn, and was completely destroyed by fire in 1853. Rebuilt a year later it produced 7,000 red shirts for General Garibaldi's volunteers.

There are nature trails in Freeholders Wood, and wooden platforms have been erected to allow splendid, unobstructed views of these falls. This pretty woodland, with its coppiced hazels, lines one bank of the Lower Falls and is a haven for wildlife. It is just a small fragment of the great forest which once filled Wensleydale, and although this comes under the management of the National Parks Authority, it is still a wood which belongs to local people, and they retain the ancient right to gather free firewood.

The Strid
WHARFEDALE

Close to Bolton Priory, the River Wharfe changes its pace and its name; it becomes The Strid and makes a headlong rush through a narrow and infamous gritstone gorge. Between its banks the water boils where pebbles of sandstone and bright, white quartz have swirled ceaselessly, wearing and enlarging the pot-holes that have been scooped in the hard rocks over ages.

At one point the ravine narrows to only four feet, and green mossy rocks reach out from either bank to hang over the torrent mid-stream. Many people have been tempted to leap across this treacherous gap, and have lost their lives in the dark and swiftly flowing river, which reaches a depth of 30 feet in places. Visitors today are warned that anyone who falls into the water here is not liable to surface for three days!

On either side of the ravine lie the 130 acres of Strid Woods; a site of 'Special Scientific Interest'. Along the marked nature trails beneath the beech, oak and sycamores, the green floor of the woodland is filled with wild flowers, and the air rings with the voices of the multitude of birds who come to nest here.

Birkdale Beck
NEAR KELD

Birkdale Beck mingles its water with those of the many little streams that tumble amongst the heather on Birkdale Moor; as they run past Keld the waters become the river Swale.

This is how the main rivers of the Dales begin, high on the Pennine watershed amongst the millstone grit and heather, or the sandstones where the water bubbles up from the mossy peat. Particularly after heavy rainfall in the hills, these boggy origins colour the clear waters of many of the rivers and streams with brown, and tint the weirs and waterfalls with gold.

The swift running waterways of the Dales are almost entirely unpolluted, and fish swim in most of the bigger streams and pools. In the dark basin below Janet's

Foss large fish can be seen leaping, and on the riverbanks people fish for trout, roach and grayling. The fish play an important part in the life cycle of the valleys, supporting colonies of mink and sometimes the rare otter. The ubiquitous heron fishes in the shallows, and sand martins and dippers feed on the insects, sweeping and darting over the waters.

Beezley Falls
INGLETON

Below the heights of Kingsdale, the River Doe flows down to the deep ravine that makes up one half of the Ingleton waterfalls area, and Beezley Falls is the first cascade of its tumultuous descent.

This spectacular series of waterfalls was not discovered until the 19th century. It was first opened to the public in 1885 – within three years the number of daily visitors exceeded 4,000, all paying a penny entrance fee.

The path that leads through the classic 'Waterfalls Walk' runs through excellent primary woodland, which is a valuable, although sadly diminishing wildlife habitat; it is the last bastion of the red squirrel in the Dales. Tawny owls and woodpeckers can be heard and little wrens and dippers dart about close to the thundering falls; in the craggy surface of the limestone, fungus and lichen flourish, revelling in the damp conditions.

Nestling at the foot of Ingleborough, the village of Ingleton is surrounded by a wealth of dramatic geological scenery, and is dominated by the 11-arched railway viaduct. Built in 1860, it was this railway that carried the first excursion trains, bringing thousands of visitors. Although the line was closed in 1954, people still flock to the village.

Semer Water
NEAR BAINBRIDGE

The calm waters of Yorkshire's largest natural lake are a magnet for anyone who enjoys water sports. Boating enthusiasts flock to Semerwater in the summer, and the sailing vessels add to the charm of the scene. The occasional hardy swimmer can sometimes be spotted braving the chilly waters, but most visitors simply come to enjoy the delightful views.

The lake was formed when a terminal moraine of boulder clay dammed the waters of a melting glacier, and the lake once reached three miles up Raydale. It is now much smaller, being only half a mile long and having a circumference of under two miles – an easy stroll. There are traces of Iron Age people in the shallows of the lake where they built houses on stilts, and Neolithic flint arrowheads have also been found.

There are three villages around Semer Water. Near its head is Marsett, a farming community gathered about a green where cattle graze; Countersett, with its strong Quaker connections, is the closest to the lake and Stalling Busk is one of the highest villages in the dales. In a field nearby is the unusual and atmospheric ruin of a tiny chapel.

Stainforth Force
RIBBLESDALE

Stainforth Force races beneath wooded banks and cascades over limestone steps as it rushes to join the River Ribble. The waterfall and the deep dark pool it has created can be reached by a footpath leading from a bridge which spans the river. This packhorse bridge was built in about 1670 to replace the 'stony ford' which was part of an ancient drove road linking York and Lancaster, and gave Stainforth its name.

The pleasant village has some limewashed houses and a small green, where a footpath leads along the side of Stainforth Beck overlooked by Langliffe Scar. Below this rests 'Samson's Toe', a large dark erratic rock perched on a narrow pedestal, and similar to those found at Norber. Stainforth's hidden second waterfall is reached here. Catrigg Force hurtles through a narrow chasm, plunging 60 feet in all, and during the winter some spectacular ice formations develop. Closely surrounded by trees this presents a magical sight in this 'secret' Dales location.

Thornton Force
INGLETON

The many delightful waterfalls of the Ingleton Glens are made up of the mingled waters of two rivers. Thornton Force is the highest waterfall here, sited above a cool, wooded gorge full of wildly rushing cascades.

This is a geologically fascinating area, and many people come here to study the rocks which reveal so much about the formation of this landscape, even to the uninformed. At Thornton Force, the River Twiss pours over a limestone ledge which was formed over primeval slate. The slate was folded and compressed many centuries ago, while the Earth was still taking shape. When the limestone was evolving, this slate had already been eroded and worn over long ages.

Where the cataract falls, the thick layer of limestone can be seen quite clearly, resting on the vertical planes of slates of the wide pool below, and it is thrilling to consider that anyone standing on this ledge, stands on rock that is 300 million years old.

Tree and River Ure
WENSLEYDALE

The fascinating knotted roots of this tree lace themselves firmly about the rocks, here on the banks of the River Ure.

This river passes through an amazing range of scenery on its journey down to the sea. It begins as a little beck, bubbling out of the bleak moorland at Mallerstang, where it is soon joined by countless others. The young river finds its way through the dark and terrifying depths of the gorge beneath Hell Gill bridge, and through the bustling village of Hawes to meander on through the broad valley of Wensleydale. Passing herds of cattle browsing contentedly in verdant meadows, it winds onwards to cascade down the wide steps of Aysgarth Falls.

Flowing more serenely out into the valley again, it passes below Bolton Castle, which has watched over this river for centuries, as it makes its way towards the pleasant market town of Leyburn. Here, the Ure sweeps southwards through the softer, flatter landscape which spreads out towards Ripon and eventually meets the Ouse.

The Ure name vanishes, but these mingled waters continue to flow on through historic York before they roll out to the Humber estuary.

Swinner Gill
SWALEDALE

Close to Keld, the highest and most remote village of Swaledale, Swinner Gill plunges for a mile down a ravine to join the river where it sweeps towards Muker. At the top of the gill is a small cave, hidden behind the falls, where Catholics would meet and pray during the days of religious persecution; at the foot there is a small ford and the remains of Beldi smelt mill, for this was an area of great lead mining activity.

The high path to Keld passes here, and can be seen as a white limestone ribbon running below the shell of long-deserted Crackpot Hall. The once-lively house is surrounded by all the evidence of the lead mining which undermined its foundations and led to its ruin.

From Swinner Gill, the tree-lined ravine at Keld can be seen, and here there are more waterfalls, and many footpaths that pass by Keld, which is hidden away amongst the green hills below the high moors. This austere little collection of houses was probably inhabited by miners and owes its present popularity with visitors to its beautiful and interesting surroundings.

Wain Wath Force

NEAR KELD

Beyond the little village of Keld is a bleak wilderness of boggy, windswept moorland, and here the little streams which will become the River Swale, gather together before tumbling over a series of falls along the valley.

North of Keld, Wain Wath is the highest of the falls, tumbling below many old mine workings, and presided over by the impressive limestone ridge of Cotterby Scar. The water here spreads and plunges into a still pool below, before it flows on to East Gill Force.

This is a pleasant and picturesque waterfall. Flanked by the rocky cliff on one side, and bright springy turf on the other, it hurries down broad steps of limestone, glinting and sparkling in dappled sunlight.

The stream takes an abrupt turn at the foot of Kisdon Hill where Kisdon Force makes two falls. Hung about with trees and wildflowers, this is the most memorable of Keld's waterfalls, for the water originally flowed on the other side of Kisdon.

A glacial dam caused it to change its route, and the strong flowing waters breached the hard rocks here to gush through the gully; the lower falls at Kisdon are their last tumultuous leap before the water reaches the valley floor.

West Burton Falls
BISHOPDALE

West Burton Village is considered by some to be the most attractive in the Dales and has a timeless and peaceful atmosphere. Many of its lovely old houses were once miners' cottages, and surround a wide green where children play in safety, for this village is well off the main road and there is no through route for cars. The village has never had a market or a church. The obelisk on the green dates from 1820 and probably replaces a much older one.

West Burton has some very pretty waterfalls which are situated conveniently close to the village. Walden Beck races down from a height of over 2,300 feet on Buckden Pike and plunges down a narrow limestone gorge to the north of West Burton.

Birds flit about the banks where ferns and ivy proliferate, and in the spring wildflowers bloom above clear rock pools. There is a ruined dam, an old corn mill and, below the falls, is a packhorse bridge; all contribute to an idyllic and bewitching scene.

ABBEYS & CASTLES

The Yorkshire Dales boast some of the most atmospheric, enchanting and complete ruined abbeys and castles in England. These historic remains are now preserved under the protection of the National Parks Authority.

Marrick Priory
SWALEDALE

The remains of Marrick Priory lie in seclusion, below the wooded slopes of Swaledale. Half a mile from Marrick village, the priory can be reached by a stone causeway known as the 'Nuns Steps'.

Not long after the Benedictine and Cistercian orders of monks came to the Yorkshire Dales, the nuns started to arrive, and in Swaledale two nunneries were built. The one at Ellerton no longer exists, but Marrick Priory's few remains can still be seen.

During the period of the Dissolution there was wholesale destruction of religious buildings but, unusually, this priory escaped. The nuns made a long and courageous stand which lasted for five years, until they were finally forced to leave.

There was no deliberate destruction of the priory and the building simply fell into decay through neglect, some parts later being incorporated into a nearby farmhouse. Although the priory tower was left untouched the church was completely rebuilt in 1811. The chapel is used as a field study centre now, but Marrick Priory is not open to the general public. However, this area is idyllic to visit and enjoy the peace and tranquillity which the women of the original priory must have found here so long ago.

Bolton Castle
WENSLEYDALE

Bolton Castle stands solidly four square, occupying a magnificent position high above Wensleydale. It was built in 1397 by Sir Richard Scrope, and as it was never expected to be used for defensive purpose he ensured that it had many domestic comforts. The Scropes were powerful aristocrats of Norman descent, and Sir Richard became an MP and Chancellor of the Exchequer. Scrope is pronounced Scroop and a character of this name who features in Shakespeare's Henry IV was probably a member of the family.

Mary, Queen of Scots was imprisoned here for almost two years, although imprisonment is hardly the correct term, for she brought a retinue of about 60 members of her household, and carts groaning with the weight of her possessions. The Castle was besieged by Cromwell's troops in 1645 and finally starved into submission. After the Civil War it remained unoccupied for more than 300 years.

Today it is being given a new lease of life by the present Lord Bolton. His main preoccupation currently, is the establishment of a parterre – or formal garden – immediately in front of the castle where there will be a rose garden, a walled herb garden, a maze and a vineyard.

Barden Tower
WHARFEDALE

Medieval Barden Tower was built by Lord Henry Clifford, who was called 'The Shepherd Lord'; as a child he lived in exile in Cumbria during the Wars of the Roses, and was raised with a shepherd's family.

Although he built Barden Tower as a hunting lodge, Lord Henry, who was a scholarly man, preferred to live here in Barden's pleasant situation by the Wharfe, rather than at Skipton Castle. In 1513 at the age of 60, Lord Henry led Craven men at the Battle of Flodden where they helped to rout the Scots, and the Clifford family still keeps the halberd which he carried into battle.

Lord Henry's descendant was Lady Anne Clifford, who spent much of her childhood here, and renovated Barden Tower along with many other buildings, after the Civil War.

This is a lovely part of Wharfedale but the river can rise dramatically quickly. The elegant Barden bridge is these days well bolstered to withstand tremendous floods, for in 1673 it was entirely swept away, along with six other bridges on the Wharfe.

The atmospheric ruins in their green and tranquil setting make a wonderful scene, and artists have always flocked here, most famously Turner and Girtin.

Bolton Priory
WHARFEDALE

Bolton Priory is often erroneously called Bolton Abbey, but was built as a priory for Augustinian canons, known as 'Black Canons'. They came to this idyllic spot on a bend of the river Wharfe after more than 30 years at Embsay. The priory was founded in 1151 by Alice de Romille; it took a hundred years to complete. A short distance further south there are the treacherous waters of the Strid, and there is a story that she had the priory established in memory of her son, whose life was claimed by the infamous torrent.

Many years later, Prior Moon was adding a west tower when the Dissolution of the Monasteries began. He attempted to bribe Henry VIII's lieutenant but failed, and the monks were evicted. The building fell into ruins, and some of the stones were taken to build local houses.

The chancel is open to the sky, but the nave survives as the parish church and the splendour of the east window remains. These romantic ruins set in an exquisite pastoral landscape of woods and parkland, have drawn some of our most famous artists to try to capture its essence on canvas.

Brough Castle
NEAR KIRKBY STEPHEN

Situated on a grassy hill, all that remains of Brough castle and its chequered history are the 12th-century keep and enclosure wall. Although it lies outside the Yorkshire Dales National Park, the castle is historically connected with the Dales through Lady Anne Clifford of Skipton Castle.

There was once a Norman fortress here, built in 1095 by William Rufus, the son of the Conqueror, on the northern part of the Roman fortress of Vertrae. The Scots destroyed it in 1174 but it was rebuilt 30 years later. It was inherited by Lady Anne Clifford in the 17th century.

Lady Anne is remembered as a philanthropist, who had a great interest in the common people of the Dales. This doughty lady, who grew up at Barden tower, became a legend for her endless and tireless travels on horseback, visiting the many castles which she owned. The Clifford family

suffered greatly during the Civil War when the Parliamentarians confiscated their properties. After the war, Lady Anne set about a great rebuilding programme, for as well as Brough, she owned the castles at Skipton, Brougham, Appleby and Pendragon Castle at Mallerstang.

After her death, Brough was allowed to fall into ruins but these remains have now been declared a National Monument, and are being preserved for posterity.

Fountains Abbey
NEAR RIPON

Fountains Abbey lies resplendent on grassy banks beside the little river Skell, which joins the Ure at Ripon, three miles away. The abbey was founded by a group of thirteen Benedictine monks who had rejected what they perceived to be the soft lifestyle of their abbey in York, in favour of the rigours of the Cistercian order.

Surrounded by thorn bushes and living in the shelter of trees and rocks, the monks would certainly have found the harsh way of life that they sought. They set about clearing the land, and the building of their abbey was completed in 1132. Fountains Abbey became the wealthiest abbey in Britain, due mainly to its trade in wool. The monks bought enormous numbers of sheep and cattle, which grazed on its farms or 'granges' that were spread across the southern dales as far west as Lancashire. Evidence of the one million acres once owned by the abbey can still be seen in place names such as Fountains Fell near Malham.

Fountains Abbey was a victim of the Dissolution and eventually fell into decay, but the glorious remains of this once great monastery should hardly be called ruins – so much still stands to delight the eye.

Easby Abbey
NEAR RICHMOND

The extensive ruins of Easby Abbey stand on a grassy bank overlooking the River Swale about a mile from Richmond. It was built in 1152 for Premonstratensian canons, who were of a similar order to the Cistercians, and in the 14th century it came into the hands of the powerful Scrope family.

The abbey was first damaged by marauding Scots and suffered further in 1346, in attacks of vandalism perpetrated by English soldiers who were billeted here. Little is left of the monastic church, but the walls of the refectory built in 1300 still stand tall, displaying some beautiful windows. The gate house also remains. An ornamental screen which came from Easby Abbey, can be seen in Wensley church.

St Agatha's church at Easby is much older than the abbey and has a plaster cast of an eighth-century cross, the original is now in the British Museum. This is a marvellous example of Anglo-Saxon sculpture depicting Christ and the Apostles on the front, with animals on the back. This church also has some well preserved 13th-century paintings on the chancel wall, and a Norman font.

Richmond Castle
SWALEDALE

When William the Conqueror had finally crushed the rebellious north, he divided the confiscated lands between his followers, determined to put an end to insurrection. Earl Alan Rufus, built his castle in its dramatic position, on a towering crag which hangs high over the fast-flowing River Swale.

The castle dates from about 1080, and one of the oldest parts to be seen today is Scolland's Hall, named after the Earl's steward. This is the oldest surviving Great Hall in England. A century later the keep was built and still stands at 100 feet high. It gives a birds eye view of the surrounding countryside, essential at a time when this stronghold suffered frequent attacks from the Scots.

Troops were garrisoned here continuously until the early twentieth century. There is a legend that King Arthur and his knights are sleeping with their treasure somewhere below Richmond, and some soldiers with an interest in the treasure once persuaded their small drummer boy to go down into the old passages. Afraid of meeting Arthur's ghost, the soldiers stayed above ground, following the sound of the boy's drumbeat. Just outside the town the beating stopped abruptly and the boy was never seen again. King Arthur slumbers on.

Skipton Castle
AIREDALE

In 1138, William Fitzduncan, a nephew of the King of Scotland, attacked Skipton Castle; however he later fell in love with and married the Norman Alice de Romille, whose family owned the castle. Afterwards it saw peace for almost 500 years.

It became thereafter the property of the Clifford family, during whose occupancy the Civil War broke out, and Cromwell's troops laid siege to many castles. At Skipton, Sir John Mallory resisted all attempts to take over the castle for three years, and with 300 men. They were eventually starved into submission and it was not for five years that Lady Anne Clifford was able to return to her battered home.

She restored many of her castles in the area over the next 25 years, but many are again in ruins today. However, at Skipton, the imposing result of her dedicated work still stands in a perfect state of preservation: the word 'Desormais' set over the gate, and meaning 'Henceforth' was perhaps prophetic.

The busy market town which stands at the gates of the castle, was a settlement long before the Normans came – Bronze Age graves have been found here. Today it is a very busy market town, of interesting, cobbled back streets and a mixture of buildings, some dating from the 14th century.

Jervaulx Abbey
NEAR MIDDLEHAM

Founded in 1156, Jervaulx Abbey was home to monks of the Cistercian order for almost four centuries, and its remains lie here still, imbued with the peace and solitude which these men sought so long ago. In 1537 this abbey, like so many others at the time, fell victim to Henry VIII's Dissolution. Its Abbot, Adam Sedbar was hanged at Tyburn for his part in the revolt known as 'The Pilgrimage of Grace', his actions also brought exceptionally ferocious destruction on his abbey.

Although almost totally in ruins, the ground plans are clearly visible today and on the grassy floor of the chapter house its elegant pillars still stand. The splendour of the great dormitory wall with its lancet windows, and 'night stair', dominates the scattered fragments of this mellow ruin, where there are fifteen different mason's marks to be found. These worn stones strewn amongst the riot of shrubs and wildflowers, are a haunting testimony to the ancient way of life that was once followed here.

Jervaulx lacks the spectacle and grandeur of some other, more complete abbey ruins, but in this peaceful setting, surrounded by the outstanding countryside of the area, it offers a rare, romantic charm.

LANDSCAPES

The Dales has some of the most dramatic and interesting geological features
of a glaciated, limestone landscape in Britain. It has drawn visitors from
around the world for more than 200 years.

The Buttertubs
NEAR THWAITE

The 'Buttertubs' are a great cluster of gaping sink holes in Upper Swaledale where the water from the bogs of Great Shunner Fell drains into the limestone.

These sink holes can be seen on both sides of the 1,726-foot high mountain pass road that runs from Thwaite to Hawes in Wensleydale. From the heart-stopping heights there is an awesome and thrilling vista of the fells and along the length of Swaledale. Stopping places on the route allow access to the deepest shafts which are situated on the eastern side, however great care should be taken as the sheer walls plummet to a depth of up to 90 feet.

At one time, the people of Thwaite travelled to the weekly market in Hawes to sell their butter and cheese, and it is said that on the homeward journey over the pass, they would lower any unsold merchandise into the cool and shady depths of these shafts, by means of baskets and ropes. The highly perishable goods would thus be preserved until the outward journey the following week. This could be how the Buttertubs came to be named, although the moniker may originate more mundanely from the shape of the limestone columns which resemble old buttertubs.

Ingleborough Peak
RIBBLESDALE

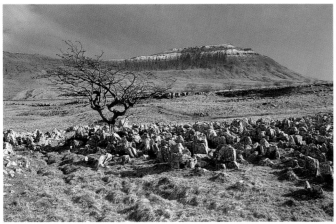

Ingleborough, rising majestically to a height of 2,373 feet, has some of the most impressive limestone features in the Dales. One of the famous 'Three Peaks', its height and astonishing variety of exciting caverns entice people from all over the world. Its distinctive tiers demonstrate the mixture of impervious and porous rocks, and it is the latter which has led to the formation of a multitude of pot-holes and caves. The most famous cave is named after the hill, and people have been coming here since it became a show cave in 1837. The legendary Gaping Gill has also drawn many intrepid pot-holers to explore its depths.

At Ingleborough's summit there are the remains of Britain's highest Iron Age fort, and close to this, ancient hut circles are evident. On the

northern point remain some intriguing stone walls of a house, which was probably built by Vikings; packhorse trails can also be found

here. The great Pennine Way runs here too, bringing many enthusiasts to walk, run and even cycle across this wild and dangerous place.

The Anvil
BRIMHAM ROCKS

The Anvil stands dramatically silhouetted against the sky, one of a group of strangely shaped rocks on Brimham Moor.

The Domesday Book records this area as a forest, but the trees were cleared by the monks of Fountains Abbey when they first began to farm the land here. This early example of 'farming vandalism' exposed the millstone-grit outcrops and, over just a few hundred years, wind and rain, frost and ice have carved some fantastic shapes.

The rocks cover an area of about 50 acres, rising clear above the purple moor, and have attracted tourists since the 18th century. Some stand 20 feet high, and their dark and twisted forms make this look like a gallery of surreal modernistic sculptures.

Walking around these shapes it is easy to see why particular rocks have acquired their popular names, such as the 'Sphinx', 'Dancing Bear', 'Blacksmith' and the astonishing 'Idol'. The latter is a huge rock balancing on an impossibly small pedestal measuring only a foot across.

Kilnsey Crag
FROM THE PARK, WHARFEDALE

Although at 170 feet it is certainly not one of the highest features in the Dales, Kilnsey Crag is one of the best known landmarks, looming abruptly above the broad flatness of Wharfedale, and overlooking the village of Conistone across the Wharfe.

The crag leans out towards the road which runs between the river and a little beck bubbling at its foot, its ominous overhanging profile all that remains of a great spur of limestone which has been truncated and undercut by the grinding flow of glaciers. Now, it dominates the green meadows where once in ages past, a great lake glittered. The ancient green track of Mastiles Lane, which once linked Fountains Abbey with its lands to the west, runs by and the old pack horse road is still used by walkers today.

Here, Kilnsey Park Lake reflects the cottages of the small village which huddles in the shadow of the crag which, with its 40-foot overhang, is a magnet for climbing and abseiling enthusiasts, as well as film-makers.

Limestone Pavements
RIBBLESDALE

The Limestone pavements of the Yorkshire Dales are probably its most significant feature, and can be found right across the massive limestone plateau. Some of the most extensive and best-known pavements can be seen at Malham and Southerscales Scars.

The surface of these platforms appears to be devoid of plant life, but closer inspection will reveal the scab-like patches of lichen which are generally light grey in colour. These lichens eat into the limestone, softening the sharper edges.

Over time, soil generally builds up on bare rock, but in thousands of years this has not happened on these outcrops. Water and acid rain has dissolved the limestone, causing the grikes, and these deep and shady fissures are a haven for plants which grow untroubled by the vagaries of the weather and browsing sheep or rabbits. Harts tongue ferns and spleenworts, wood anemones and wood sorrel are all associated with damp and sheltered woodland and yet they flourish in this dry and apparently soil-less environment.

The trees that manage to grow on the pavements, are stunted by the struggle to survive, and their dark twisted forms add a surreal touch to the stark and barren rock of these lunar landscapes.

Norber Erratic
NEAR AUSTWICK

A testament to the power of the glaciers, the Norber erratics can be seen high on the limestone hillside above the village of Austwick, where they have stood, unmoving, for the 12,000 years since the end of the last Ice Age.

Erratics are rocks and boulders that were carried great distances from their original position by the moving ice sheets, and deposited in distant and very different situations. Geologists believe that these boulders at Norber probably came from Crummack Dale (about half a mile away) as there are outcrops of the same dark Silurian gritstone on the valley floor there.

There are hundreds of these ancient and sombre erratics at Norber, some of which measure up to ten feet across, contrasting strangely with the much younger white limestone. Together these create an almost primeval landscape. The 'mushrooms' were formed over long ages: the hard rock of the erratics protected the limestone beneath, while the surrounding area was weathered and eroded away; the small area of limestone under each boulder was thus preserved, forming a plinth on which these intriguing geological features seem to balance.

Malham Cove
NEAR MALHAM

Many visitors are drawn to the splendid limestone pavements which top the crag at Malham, extending for 1,000 feet. This soaring limestone cliff, that dominates the sweeping curve of Malham Cove, was formed 330 million years ago. Subsequent glaciation, alternating with warmer periods and slightly acid rainfall, dissolved the limestone, forming the clints and runnels which are the features of these pavements.

Aeons ago, a mighty waterfall plunged from the Watlowes Valley above the crag, its height exceeding that of Niagara Falls. All trace of this great cataract has disappeared and now only little Malham beck trickles along the valley floor, and meanders peacefully through the village, out of all proportion to the majesty of the crag.

Malham tarn on the moor above the cliff is an upland lake unusually formed in the porous limestone because of its impervious slate bed. Charles Kingsley came to walk here and to fish, and he found the inspiration for his 19th-century fairy tale, *The Water Babies* in the little beck.

From the tarn there is a descent through the now dry, boulder-strewn Watlowes Valley, which ends at the broad limestone plateau with its magnificent vista of upper Airedale.

Penyghent Peak
NEAR HORTON-IN-RIBBLESDALE

The steep southern 'nose' and sloping top make Penyghent easily recognisable, crouching over the flat limestone moors which surround it. Rising to 2,273 feet, this is the lowest of the trio of mountains which make up the 'Three Peaks' area of the Yorkshire Dales, and it is at Horton below Penyghent, that the famous Three Peaks Race begins and ends.

The climb to the flat, millstone grit summit is not strenuous. The Pennine Way leads over Penyghent, and those who venture here are well rewarded. The flatter parts of this hill are dotted with pot-holes, most famously 'Great Hunt Pot', while the craggy rocks are hung about with the glorious colour of purple saxifrage.

The views are quite breathtaking; a panoramic vista rolls out in all directions. Ingleborough and Whernside peaks loom up across the Ribble valley, Langstrothdale lies further to the north, and to the south-east is Fountains Fell, where the Pennine Way runs on.

Reef Knoll Limestone Boulder
RIBBLESDALE

This boulder bears a similarity to the dark gritstone erratics of Norber, however, this rock is formed from limestone, and its curious relief markings indicate that it was once part of a coral reef. When this land was covered by the shallow tropical seas that eventually formed the limestone, the warm carboniferous waters provided the ideal environment for the corals, which grew around its islands.

Many ages later these were covered by softer types of limestone and other rocks, and as the seas receded these were subject to quicker erosion. As they have been worn down, the hard reefs of coral have been exposed, especially to the south. This erosion and exposure is still going on, and these reefs will in time become more pronounced.

In Wharfedale near Thorpe, the hills of Kail, Ebolton, Stebden and Butter Haw rise up in a circle, a splendid example of reef knolls just being revealed, and providing a thought-provoking reminder of the warm lagoons and the life that teemed in them here, aeons ago.

Oxnop Scar
ABOVE ASKRIGG

The immense row of limestone crags above Oxnop Moor gleams in the sunlight, and the steep hillside drops below, littered with the scree and boulders which have been loosened by water and frost, to tumble down from the great outcrop.

Oxnop Scar stands 500 feet above sea level, and few people venture far from the high pass road which links Swaledale with Wensleydale. From the highest point of the road there are magnificent views: to the north lies Muker and the solitary building of 17th-century Low Oxnop Hall; it is certainly the most remarkable building of this period in Swaledale. To the south the moorland rolls down to Askrigg, its church rising clearly above the cottages, and Semer Water lake glitters in the far distance. Those who pause here may be rewarded by a glimpse of the golden plovers that find safe nesting sites in this undisturbed and awesome place.

Long Churn
INGLEBOROUGH

Water dives into many pot-holes of the Three Peaks district, mysteriously re-appearing in distant caves. In the days before electricity, when candles were the only source of light, these black, cavernous depths were generally given a wide berth, but there were some whose sense of adventure overcame their fear of the unknown, as long ago as the 18th century.

When the first tourists came to the Yorkshire Dales, guides would escort parties down into Long Churn on Ingleborough's slopes. They carried wooden ladders, and the blackening of the rocks in this long and winding series of caves, indicate the route these people took, carrying flaming torches. At this time the various features of these caverns were given names such as 'Dr Bannister's Handbasin' and 'St Paul's'.

This underground system was found to connect with Diccan Pot and Alum Pot which was discovered in 1847. The first people to descend into this cave used a fire escape belt and ropes and pulleys to get out. A year later, navvies who were working on the nearby Settle to Carlisle railway line erected an enormous wooden gantry over the shaft, enabling these early cavers to be lowered and raised in a large bucket.

Gordale Scar
NEAR MALHAM

Close to Malham Cove and Janet's Foss is a wide, boulder-strewn meadow and broad sky where the Gordale Scar gorge opens. At first seeming quite innocuous, dramatic limestone walls soon close in, and at the narrow head of the ravine the sheer cliffs close in ominously overhead.

It is sometimes thought that the gorge was formed when the roof of a great cave fell in, but the more probable explanation is that it was scoured out of the rocks by glacial meltwater carrying abrasive rocks and sediments.

Rocks are still occasionally hurled down here, loosened by the action of frost, and the cold and threatening atmosphere of this place has made a deep impression on its many visitors, including Turner and Wordworth. The romantic poet Thomas Gray came here in the 18th century and was reportedly quite terrified.

Rocks and boulders are piled steeply at the narrowest point of Gordale, over which a waterfall tumbles down. It varies in size, disappearing completely during dry periods, and the rocks can usually be climbed to reach the top. Now there are steps and footpaths, where the people of Malham used to graze their hardy and sure-footed little goats.

Limestone Gorge
RIVER DEE, GARSDALE

The waters of the River Dee, constantly washing over the layers of weaker shales, have created the attractive staircase effect of shallow waterfalls in the hard limestone of the river bed, and here the action of pebbles and swirling water has scooped hundreds of little hollows in the rock.

This is one of the many interesting features along the Adam Sedgewick Trail, named after the great Victorian geologist who was born in Dent, a short distance to the south. He discovered and studied the Dent Fault, which is one of the two great faults in the geological systems of the Yorkshire Dales.

Faults are enormous fractures made by ancient upheavals in the land mass, which then led to the slipping of one side so revealing the strata of rocks as they were laid down millions of years ago. The Craven Fault is actually a line of three faults which can be detected to the south of Ingleborough, at Giggleswick Scar and Malham Cove.

To the west is the Dent Fault where the more ancient Silurian slates of the Lake District meet the carboniferous limestone and Yoredale shales of the Dales; the Adam Sedgwick trail follows a fascinating route showing some of the fault's remarkable geology.

Whernside
RIBBLESDALE

Whernside marks the highest point in the Dales, and its massive bulk towers 2,415 feet over the Dales Way Path, dwarfing the Ribblehead Viaduct below. The viaduct was constructed using limestone hewn from the foot of Whernside.

Composed mainly of impervious gritstone, there are several small tarns to be found on the flanks of this mountain, but there are none of the spectacular pot-holes of Ingleborough or Penyghent. Its chief importance is to the experienced fell walkers, who relish the challenge of reaching its cold and breezy heights, and to its role as part of the Three Peaks Race.

Walkers flock here for the annual race to climb all three peaks of the area, Ingleborough, Penyghent and Whernside, in one day. Fell runners can complete this route within four hours, but most walkers take 10 to 12 hours. This is not for the novice, for dangers abound in this spectacular area, and there is a 'clocking-in' system in force to ensure that all the participants return safely.

CUSTOMS & LEGENDS

The customs and legends of the Dales are rooted in its history and landscape. Pagan and Christian rituals are still celebrated, ghosts and trolls were said to inhabit dark caverns, and it is believed giants once occupied the soaring crags.

Hubberholme Churchyard
WHARFEDALE

Sheep graze placidly in the churchyard of St Michael, Hubberholme. Inside the little church is a plaque to the memory of J. B. Priestley, the well known author of *The Good Companions*, *An Inspector Calls* and many other works. He delighted in this church and his ashes were placed here in the graveyard.

There is a sense of timelessness all around this quiet village as the local people go about their work tending their flocks; in June and July they can be seen in the meadows, gathering hay for winter feed as generations have done before them.

Every New Year the Hubberholme Parliament sits to hold a 'candle auction'. Next to the inn, which was once the vicarage, the church owns some land known as the 'Poor Pasture', which the local farmers bid to rent for one year. The parliament consists of the 'Lords' or the lounge bar where the auctioneer (once the vicar) sits; the farmers sit in the public bar which is the 'Commons'. A candle is lit and bidding lasts until it burns out. This is a very serious auction for the land is needed, and the rent money is given to the poor.

Simon Seat
BARDEN FELL

The cluster of crags and rocks at the summit of Barden Fell provides a wonderful viewpoint above Skyreholme, which is a tributary valley of the Wharfe. There is a story that relates how a shepherd tending his flocks on Barden moor, found a baby amongst these rocks. He took the child home where, despite their poverty, the other shepherds agreed to help with the raising of the boy, each putting a little money into a fund. The child was named Simon after the man who had found him, and he acquired the surname Amang'em because the shepherds had shared his upbringing 'among them.'

Barden moor is a wild and exhilarating place to explore, but below it to the south, in contrast are the green and pleasant environs of Bolton Priory and the sheltered climate of Strid woods. Immediately beneath the high fell is Posforth Gill, in medieval times this area was an old deer park. Now it is called 'The Valley of Desolation' because it was once laid waste by a great landslip. Time passed and although the valley recovered to become a very pleasant place, it still retains its ominous-sounding name.

The Burning of Owd Bartle

WEST WITTON

It is said that a wicked giant once inhabited the heights of Pen Hill above West Witton, but he met his end when the ghost of a young girl that he had slaughtered caused his own great dog to attack him, sending him over the precipice.

These days the people of West Witton enjoy their annual festivities untroubled by any evil presence. On the nearest Saturday to the 24th August the villagers celebrate with a 'feast' or festival, when gardens are opened to the public and there is a 'fell race' up Pen Hill. In the evening, a huge bonfire is lit for 'The Burning of Owd Bartle', when an effigy is burned. The 24th August is St Bartholomew's feast day, although the custom probably has its origins in pre-Christian times.

The cottages of West Witton were once dotted solely along the high roadside, but the rising population during the 18th and 19th centuries, has resulted in a continuous linear village that stretches for almost a mile. The old road to West Burton and a field path provide a pleasant walk up to the 1,844-feet-high summit of Pen Hill, and one of the most breathtaking aerial views in the Dales.

Leyburn Shawl
LEYBURN

The path behind the grand ancient house of Thornborough Hall in Leyburn leads out onto a ridge of grass and trees known as 'The Leyburn Shawl'. This provides a splendid platform, looking out on a spectacular view of Wensleydale, with seats to allow visitors the luxury of lingering in comfort. The walk was laid out in the last century, and became a fashionable promenade. The famed 'Leyburn Tea Festival' took place here, and attracted great crowds; in 1845 more than 3,000 people came to enjoy the tea and dancing.

There are several paths to follow from the Shawl, all of which afford very pleasant walks. One of these runs through the Bolton Park Estate and on to Bolton Castle and its village. 'Queen's Gap' is said to be the place where Mary, Queen of Scots was recaptured after escaping from Bolton Castle where she had been imprisoned. Stories of her escape also allege that, as she fled, she dropped her shawl, thus giving the place its name.

Hornblower
BAINBRIDGE

The Bainbridge horn-blower wears his uniform to blow his horn at nine o'clock every evening. It is said that the sound of the horn guided travellers to the safety of the village after dark, in the days when packs of wolves ran in the forests hereabouts. The custom probably has less philanthropic origins, however. After the Conquest, the Normans began to seize land all over Yorkshire including great tracts of what is now the Yorkshire Dales. The people took great exception to this appropriation, and resisted strongly. The rebellion was ferociously put down during the 'Harrying of the North' which reached parts of the Dales, and the people suffered terrible persecution. In establishing their authority, the Norman rulers introduced measures to control the population, including curfews to curtail poaching in their hunting preserves.

Some of these rules have been passed on as customs which continue to be preserved today. An example of this is the blowing of three blasts on the Bainbridge curfew horn, which has been carried out by several generations of the Metcalfe family.

Bridge over the Bain
SEMERWATER

This triple-arched bridge spans the river Bain, the shortest river in the Dales. It is the outflow for the largest natural lake in the Dales: Semer Water, whose calm beauty has provided a spiritual and artistic inspiration for many.

In 1956, the vicar of Askrigg held the first open air service here from a 'floating pulpit'; this continues today. On the Sunday of every August Bank Holiday weekend, the vicar stands in a boat and preaches to a congregation gathered on the shores.

Turner came here frequently, and his watercolour of Semerwater (or Simmer Lake as he knew it) is now in the British Museum. In the centre of the foreground of the picture is a huge boulder, this is the Carlin stone which rests on the lake's shores, and is reputed to have been thrown by the devil – though geologists claim it was deposited by a glacier.

A beautiful city is said to have stood here, but was drowned after a curse. It is claimed that sometimes, when the lake is still and silent, the ringing of bells can be heard coming from the city beneath the water.

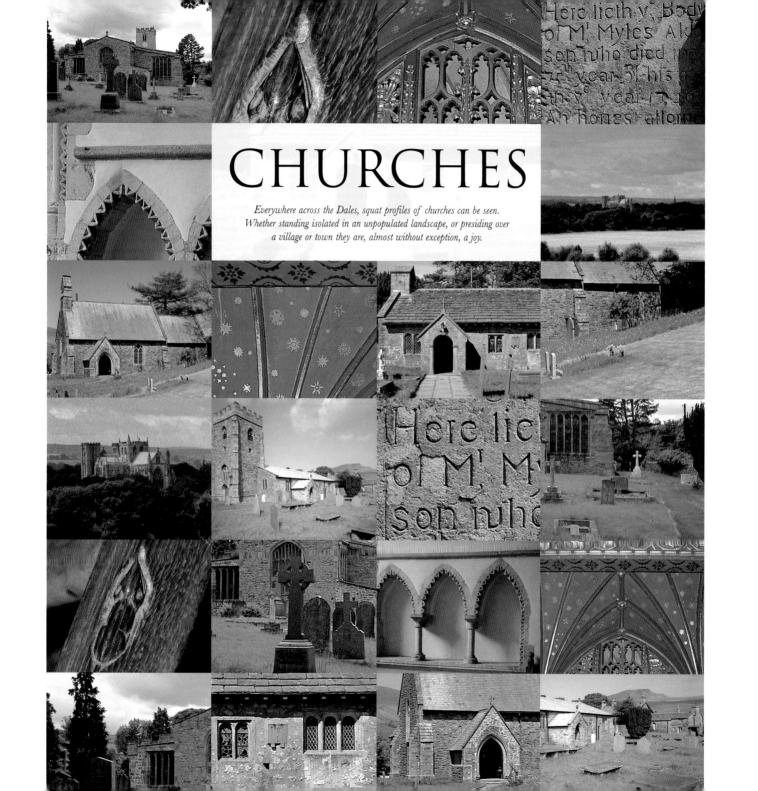

CHURCHES

Everywhere across the Dales, squat profiles of churches can be seen. Whether standing isolated in an unpopulated landscape, or presiding over a village or town they are, almost without exception, a joy.

St Andrew's Church
GRINTON

The extensive parish of Grinton once covered the whole of Swaledale, and for the people who travelled miles to the Sunday services, a regular fair was held afterwards. There is an ancient track from Keld at the head of the dale which leads to Grinton, it is known as the 'Corpse Way'. Its name derives from the era when the deceased of remote villages and farms were carried along this path in wicker baskets to be buried in the churchyard.

St Andrew's church is probably situated on an ancient pagan site and was built by monks of Bridlington. There has been a church here for 900 years and some original features remain, although the building dates mostly from the 13th to the 15th centuries. It has all the peace and atmosphere of centuries of worship. There are some superb stained glass windows which are a mixture of Medieval and Victorian, and an intriguing narrow window is set in the wall, giving a view from outside of a side altar. This is known as the 'leper's squint' because, through this small slit, those afflicted with the disease could observe the service without entering the church and spreading the contagion.

St Leonard's Chapel
CHAPEL-LE-DALE

The exquisite little chapel of St Leonard is barely 50 feet long; it was built in the 17th century on the site on an ancient chapel of ease for Ingleton, which gave the village its name. Chapels of ease were small, subordinate churches in areas whose mother church would cover a vast and dispersed parish, as was common in the Dales at one time. There is some superb stained glass here, but most memorable is the touchingly worded plaque in honour of the hundreds of men who died building the Settle to Carlisle railway.

Christopher Long, the man who discovered the nearby White Scar Cave in 1923 is buried here. This show cave is the most impressive in the Dales, with a magnificent display of stalactites and stalagmites, some of which date back 225,000 years.

Chapel-le-Dale is tucked into the foot of Ingleborough, and nearby are many echoing caves and nightmarish pot-holes which have inevitably given rise to ghost stories. Above the church, Hurtle Pot is said to be haunted by a loathsome Boggart who drowns his victims in its waters.

St Michael's Church
HUBBERHOLME

The little village of Hubberholme is hidden away from the main highway beside the River Wharfe, but its church is renowned. There is a unique charm about St Michael and All the Angels for there is a remarkable blending of ancient and modern in its simple interior. The new window in the south wall shows, in glowing colours, the history of the parish, and the simple 20th-century oak pews were made by Robert Thompson, 'The Mouse Man of Kilburn'. It is entertaining to search for his carved 'signature' mice, which can be found running up and down the pews.

Above Robert Thompson's handiwork hangs one of the greatest treasures of the Yorkshire Dales, a splendid rood-loft. Painted red, black and gold and dating from 1558 it is one of only two to survive after an edict of 1571, which decreed that all rood-lofts should be destroyed. Hubberholme's loft escaped destruction simply because of its position in this quiet little backwater.

Originally a forest chapel, this unassuming little church is imbued with a timeless peace which made it J. B. Priestley's favourite place, and probably one of the greatest delights in the Dales.

St Oswald's Church
ASKRIGG

This weather-worn old gravestone was placed in Askrigg churchyard in 1713 and is apparently the oldest legible memorial to be found here. It has been hung on the church wall now, where it is protected from further erosion by the slates which have been set above it.

Askrigg has been settled continuously since prehistoric times, but until the building of a church here in the 12th century, the Christian population had to worship and be buried at Aysgarth. St Oswald's is a typically low-profile Dales church and is a very fine example of the perpendicular style, with a splendid vaulted tower and remarkable beamed ceiling in the nave. The north aisle was added in the 15th century, and the south aisle was restored in 1770. The zealous Victorian parishioners replaced the furnishings and added other embellishments.

In this graveyard lie those like the 'Honest Attorney' who had the worldly means to ensure the kind of immortality afforded by the old stones. Alongside them rest those countless hard-working Dalesfolk whose only memorial must be the landscape that they helped to shape.

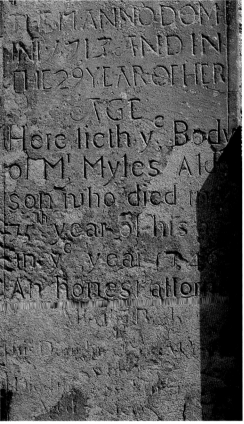

St Mark's Church
CAUTLEY

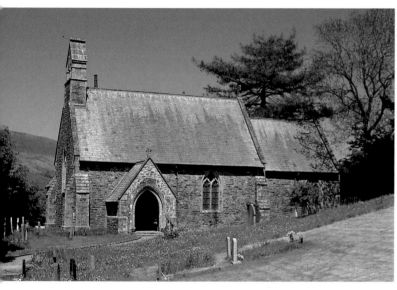

St Mark's at Cautley is a tiny church built to serve a very sparse population and is hidden away from the road, close to Cautley Spout. The immense Howgill Fells rise as a backdrop, dotted with dark trees and white sheep, making this one of the most delightfully positioned churches in the Dales.

After the arrival of the Normans, and with the establishment of the monasteries, many churches were built in the Dales. Some of these Norman churches were built on existing sites where earlier churches had stood, but before this time, one Mother Church would generally have served a huge parish. For example, Aysgarth church had a parish of 80,000 acres, and the evidence of the long distances that the faithful had to tread, can be seen in the miles of narrow footpaths which thread across the land to converge at that church.

During the Dark Ages, courageous missionaries had come to even the most remote parts of this land. They braved the wild animals who roamed the great forests here, to preach the Christian message at particular places marked by preaching crosses, and this isolated little church may well be situated where one of these once stood.

St Andrew's Church
AYSGARTH

This beautiful screen is one of two which can be seen in St Andrew's Church at Aysgarth. Originally these outstanding examples of medieval woodwork were made for Jervaulx Abbey, probably at Ripon, and were brought here after the Dissolution during which the Abbey was almost razed to the ground.

Overlooking the Upper Falls, Aysgarth Church is a typical Victorian edifice. Built in 1866 on older foundations, its four-acre churchyard is the largest in England and its great size seems incongruous in this setting. There

are only a few houses, an inn and an old mill nearby, but for centuries this was the Mother Church for a large part of Wensleydale, and a great number of footpaths converge here.

Aysgarth village is reached by a path which passes over fields above the bend in the river with a birds-eye view of the falls. The pretty village has a tiny green, on which stood the village stocks, and owes its unspoilt charm to its distance from the tourist attraction of the waterfalls.

St Oswald's Church
HORTON-IN-RIBBLESDALE

The massive scar of Beecroft Quarry looms over the village of Horton-in-Ribblesdale. Situated between Ingleborough and Penyghent, it has become a popular centre for the walkers who come along the Pennine Way, and for adventurers lured by the danger and exhilaration of the surrounding limestone countryside. This is where the various races which take place over the Three Peaks begin and end. Horton also has a very intriguing church. St Oswald's dates from Norman times as can be seen from its doorway, and was once the Mother Church for Ribblesdale. Its roof is made from Dales lead and there are some splendid examples of stained glass. Of particular note is a small and ancient depiction of Thomas à Becket.

One of the most notable features of this church is the way it leans. A glance at the angle of the pillars can seem worrying, but they have been leaning like this for generations and the building is in no danger of suddenly collapsing. A definite slant can be discerned in many east windows of the churches in the Dales, but none display an entire interior that leans as St Oswald's does.

Holy Trinity Church
WENSLEY

This fine old triple Sedilia, for the use of clergy, is set close to the altar of Holy Trinity Church in Wensley. This lovely old church was built in 1245 on the site of a Saxon church, and stones from that ancient building, dating from 760, are set in one wall. There have been some additions to Holy Trinity over the centuries, including a modern side altar, but since the raising of the chancel and aisle walls in the 15th century, the church stands much as it did 700 years ago. The only Victorian addition is the sundial.

The interior has many interesting features: 13th-century windows and heraldic shields, early 14th-century murals, a lovely ornamental 15th-century screen, and 18th-century stalls.

John Wesley preached here, and Frances l'Anson, the original 'Sweet lass of Richmond Hill', was baptised in the 17th-century font. The church's connection with Bolton Hall, whose gates are close by, began with the powerful Scrope family of Bolton Castle, long before the Dissolution; their family pew can still be seen in the church.

This is one of the most outstanding churches in the Dales, and its pale stone gleams warmly from an airy position above Wensleydale, beside the pretty cottages of Wensley village.

Ripon Cathedral
RIPON

In 672, a church was founded on the site of Ripon Cathedral in 672 by St Willfrid, its first bishop; it was razed to the ground by the Danish invaders in 860. However, the crypt survived, and still remains, chill and eerie, along a narrow tunnel beneath the Cathedral, where long ago, pilgrims queued to venerate the saint. The pilgrimage is remembered every year on St Willfrid's feast day in August, when there is a procession.

A later Norman church on this site was also ruined, and the awe-inspiring architecture which remains today to dominate the little town, was built between the 12th and 13th centuries. The building work was begun by Archbishop Roger of York, and the stupendous West Front, was added in 1220 by Archbishop Walter de Grey, using millstone grit.

The minster became a cathedral in 1836, and exhibits some outstanding woodcarvings and stained glass. The now-famous choir can be appreciated singing from the 15th-century choir stalls, during concerts which are held here regularly.

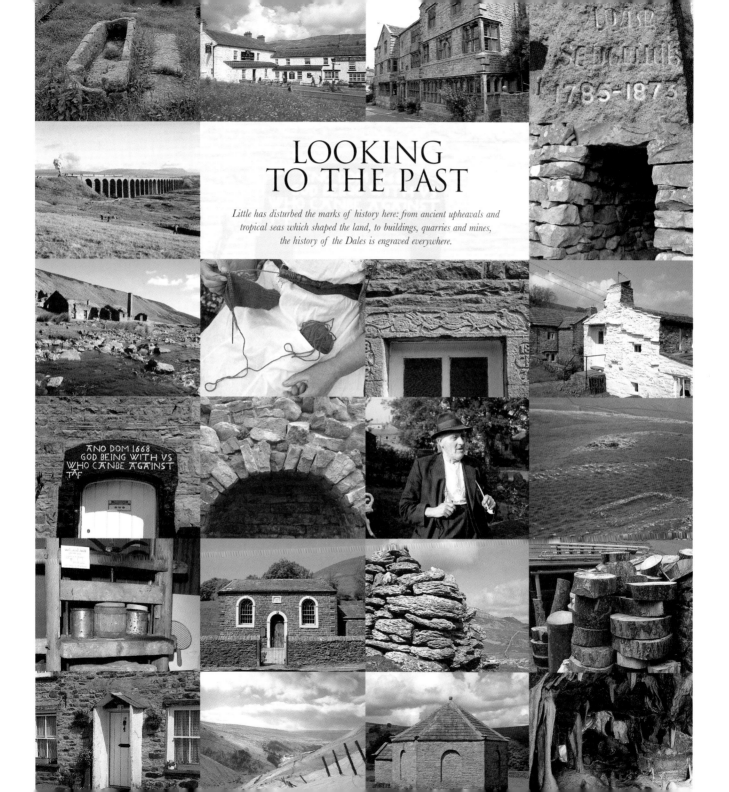

LOOKING TO THE PAST

Little has disturbed the marks of history here: from ancient upheavals and tropical seas which shaped the land, to buildings, quarries and mines, the history of the Dales is engraved everywhere.

Adam Sedgewick Memorial
DENT

On Dent's cobbled main street stands an eye-catching fountain of pink shap granite, a memorial to Dent's most famous son. The son of the local vicar, Adam Sedgewick, 'the father of modern geology', was born in 1785 at the old parsonage. He attended the grammar school here and went on to become a distinguished professor of geology at Cambridge.

There was a tremendous upsurge of interest in the natural world and the sciences during Adam's lifetime, and Victorian tourists would come to the Dales to marvel at the plethora of geological features displaying the newly understood formation of our landscapes.

Despite the dawning of scientific enlightenment, local ideas were still often firmly entrenched in prudery, and Adam Sedgewick had to exert his influence to ensure the preservation of the 'unseemly' old name of the local hamlet of Cowgill. This memorial commemorates the success of his efforts.

His true memorial as a pioneering geologist is a short path which was created in 1984 as part of the new National Parks Scheme. The 'Adam Sedgewick Trail', commemorating the 200th anniversary of his birth, runs for half a mile near Sedbergh. Along its course, the fascinating geological features of the Dent Fault are revealed.

Keartons' Cottage
THWAITE

Wildlife decorates the lintel of this cottage in Thwaite and the initials CK and RK indicate that this is where the pioneering naturalists, Cherry and Richard Kearton were born, and shows when. These famous Victorian men of Swaledale were born into a family who could trace their ancestry in the dale back to the 14th century. They attended the school in the neighbouring village of Muker, and from these humble beginnings went on to achieve great national renown, Cherry as a photographer and Richard as a lecturer and writer.

While staying near London, Cherry bought a second-hand camera and took a photograph of a thrush's nest. This was to have a catalytic effect on their lives, for it inspired Richard to write a book on birds' nests. Theirs was the first book on natural history to be illustrated with photographs and proved a great success, for it introduced a hitherto solely academic subject to the general public.

Richard and Cherry took countless photographs of the wildlife in the Dales and, as there were no telephoto lenses, they had to go to great lengths

to obtain their excellent pictures, even hanging over precipices. They also built some extraordinary hides which included artificial boulders and trees, and even stuffed cows.

Ribblehead Viaduct
RIBBLESDALE

In the shadow of the towering peaks of Ingleborough and Whernside, the Ribblehead Viaduct makes a half mile sweep over Blea moor. Twenty-four arches soar to a height of 105 feet, and those who know the force of the winds that can howl down from the nearby mountains, will appreciate the awesome achievement of the men who constructed it. There is an anecdotal story which says that one man was swept off the viaduct, under the arch and deposited back on the other side. Many others were not so fortunate. The navvies who built this magnificent structure used blocks of limestone hewn from quarries at the foot of Whernside – some of which weighed nearly eight tons.

The viaduct was opened for the Settle to Carlisle line in 1876. At the time two rival concerns were running the lines that met here and a dispute between them led to two stations being opened at either end of the viaduct, which meant that passengers who wanted to continue their journey, had what must have been a terrifying walk, to make the connection.

Celtic Wall
SMEARSETT

This remnant of an ancient Celtic wall is extremely difficult to date, for Celts are known to have journeyed from across Europe and moved into the area over a long period, starting in the 7th century BC. The first large settlements were probably established in the Yorkshire Dales in about 100 BC.

The Celts' culture flourished with the Iron Age, and they began to farm and breed horses. In the Yorkshire Dales, the turf-covered outlines of hut circles and the field enclosures of Celtic farms can be easily detected, for the land has remained untouched by the plough in many places, and the shadows cast by low sunlight throws them into sharp relief.

The most important day for the Celts was 'Samain', the fertility feast of New Year, celebrated in November. In May they celebrated the feast of Beltane, when great bonfires were lit right across the country, on high peaks such as Ingleborough where there are the remains of a wall encircling the summit.

The Romans also came here but they made little impression on the remote communities of the Dales, and when they left the Celtish culture recovered, in many ways enhanced by the laws and discipline of their erstwhile rulers.

Entrance to Lead Mine Tunnel
COGDEN MOOR

This archway is the entrance to one of the many lead mining tunnels on Cogden Moor, south of Grinton in Swaledale. The entire valley, which rises from Cogden Beck, is gashed and scarred by the 'hushes' and debris of the lead mining days when Swaledale was producing prodigious amount of the ore from its many mines.

Remains of the long flues, which replaced the earlier and shorter chimneys of the smelt mills can be seen. These became necessary when it was realised that the poisonous fumes produced by the smelting method, were drifting onto the farmland of the valleys. These long flues were also regularly cleaned, often by small boys, to lower the pollution.

The smelt mill on Cogden Moor was built by the London Lead Company in 1840, and is the only smelt mill in the Dales which is still roofed. Recent conservation work on all these remains has ensured the preservation of this very interesting living museum.

Kit Calvert
HAWES

One of the greatest Dales characters of this century, Kit Calvert was born at Burtersett near Hawes in 1903. His father worked at the flagstone quarries at Burtersett, and Kit later owned a farm close to Hawes.

His abiding interest in Wensleydale developed into an encyclopaedic knowledge of its life and history. He saw tremendous changes in the way of life here, and with his familiar clay pipe in hand, he would recount vividly stories of 'The Good Old Days'; tales of hay-making suppers, working flagstone quarries and mills, and of local characters, all long passed away.

Kit's passion for books led him to open a bookshop in Hawes, and the shop still bears his name. He also won great respect and renown when he prevented the closure of the cheesemaking factory at Hawes in 1935. He rallied local support, and his success in saving the dairy led to him being appointed the Managing Director.

In 1977 he was awarded the MBE for his lifelong dedication to Wensleydale. He died in 1984, and the many interviews that he gave will ensure that he will always be remembered as the 'Complete Dalesman'.

Cheese Press
WENSLEYDALE

This old cheese press is a reminder of the long history of cheesemaking in this, the 'Dairy Dale'.

For many years cheeses were made on the farms whose cattle grazed the lush summer pastures of this broad dale, and as far back as the 17th century they were supplying great quantities of cheese and butter to the London market. Originally made with ewes milk, this had been supplanted by cows milk by the early 19th century, producing the familiar, mild and crumbly textured cheese which has long been so popular. With the advent of the railways and a daily milk train in 1870, transportation was made much easier, and increasing demand for Wensleydale cheese led to the opening of the first cheesemaking factory in Hawes in 1897.

Inevitably, cheesemaking on the farms declined, and even the cheese factory itself has been threatened with closure. In 1930, Kit Calvert, a well known local Dalesman, saved it from being closed down, and more recently, strong, popular opposition overturned plans to move it to Lancashire. Today, visitors can still see the cheese being made in its historic setting, and enjoy sampling this 'nation's favourite'.

Cottages at Countersett
WENSLEYDALE

These pretty cottages at Countersett are typical of Wensleydale today. It is generally thought that the houses of the Dales have remained unchanged for many centuries, but in fact there have been some radical changes. The old vernacular buildings were long and narrow, with small windows and steeply thatched roofs to dispel the heavy rainfall. The living space was combined with the kitchen, making use of the warmth generated by the cooking ranges.

When a new prosperity came to these villages during the 18th century, people could afford to make their houses more comfortable.

Slates and flagstones replaced thatch everywhere, and as the new roofs did not need to be pitched so steeply, the walls of the houses could be raised. Bigger windows were put in, and very many kitchens were added on at the backs of the cottages.

New cottages sprang up too, to accommodate the miners and mill workers at this time. Whole terraces were built and dwellings were built in the gaps between the existing houses. These changes were generally very subtle, and as the same local stone was always used, they never detract from the harmonious and pleasing aspect of the villages in the Dales.

Porch with Flagstone Roof
SEDBERGH

Many years ago, when the limestone of the Yorkshire Dales was being laid down, ancient rivers flowed via deltas into the shallow seas and carried the deposits of sand and mud which eventually made up the softer layers of sandstone and mudstone which can be seen in the exposed limestone of the valley sides.

Rocks have been quarried for many years in the Dales, and many of the scars that can be seen on the hillsides are the result of the workings of early settlers. Flagstones are quarried from mudstones, siltstones and a very hard gritstone known as Greywacke. This rock splits easily into layers and is commonly known as Burtersett Flagstone, for it is at Burtersett and nearby Gayle that most of it was obtained.

The quarrying began in 1860 and ceased in about 1930 but all over the Dales flagstone tiles can be seen on roofs. It had many other uses too, such as for paving, tombstones and stiles.

The arched openings of the quarries can still be seen in the hillsides around Burtersett and Gayle, and at the height of production here in 1890, the records show that 15,000 tons of flagstone was sent to the mill towns of Lancashire.

Limekiln
NEAR SEDBERGH

The absence of arable farming in the Yorkshire Dales is due to the poverty of the soil, which makes it suitable only for pasture. As a result lime has been used here as an abundant, locally obtained fertiliser to increase the production of a few necessary crops and fodder since the 18th century. In 1774, a farmer in Langstrothdale experimented with lime on his land. First, the heather in his fields was burnt off, then the land was drained. A dressing of lime was found to greatly improve his yield of turnips and hay in successive years, and the use of lime quickly spread.

The enclosure acts of the 18th and 19th centuries frequently specified that a kiln could be built near to the outcrops of limestone close to the fields, and limekilns like this one were built all over the Dales.

Here, the rock was broken up and put into the funnel of sandstone at the top. Layered with coal or sometimes peat, it was allowed to burn slowly and the resulting fine lime was used to sweeten the soil. As limewash, it also gave a protective coating to dwellings which had been built with less weather-resistant types of stone.

Sheep Identity Marks
GUNNERSIDE FORGE, SWALEDALE

Between the pretty cottages overlooking the tree-lined beck at Gunnerside, stands the deserted and dilapidated remains of the old forge.

Outside, anvils, old tools and iron barrel hoops lie rusting quietly amongst the grass, a reminder of the days when this would have been the noisiest and busiest spot in the village. This part of Swaledale was one of the most prolific of the lead-producing areas and it is not difficult to conjure up a picture of the dark little Dales ponies who hauled the lead, waiting to be shod as the bellows made the fires roar, and the farriers hammered the shoes on the anvil.

Sheep too would be driven by, each animal being marked with its owner's branding iron before it was allowed the freedom of the common grazing land. The letters and marks burnt into the wooden door here, show where the brands were checked before use. They are much smaller than cattle brands because sheep could be branded only on their horns.

The ponies are long gone, and nowadays every sheep is marked with a colourful waterproof dye. The village blacksmith had to find work elsewhere, leaving his forge to slow decay.

Powder House
ARKENGARTHDALE

When dynamite was first used to blast through the ore-bearing rocks it improved the speed of the old method of rock drilling by two thirds, and reduced the cost by as much as a half. At Arkengarthdale the remarkable octagonal powder house, which dates from about 1804, is now the only roofed building amongst the detritus of bygone lead mining.

The octagonal smelt mill, built in the same architectural style, has unfortunately been dismantled, but the powder house remains almost perfect. It now has an idyllic setting, rising from a sea of wildflowers in a hay meadow which slopes down to the wooded banks of Arkle Beck. Eskeleth bridge adds to this charming and peaceful scene, and nearby the church of St Mary the Virgin also overlooks the beck, its gates guarded by two venerable beech trees which cast dappled shade over the Victorian graves and tombstones.

This church exudes a quiet simplicity, it has no stained glass but its fine oak altar is the work of the famous woodcarver Robert Thompson, and his trademark carved mouse can be seen on the north wall. Like the old powder house, peace and quiet prevail here, where once the sound of hundreds of men at the busy lead workings, filled the air.

Grooves on Norman Arch
ST OSWALD'S, HORTON-IN-RIBBLESDALE

The curious grooves and scratches in the stonework around the entrance to St Oswald's church are attributed to the sharpening of arrows and swords long ago. They can be seen only around the main doorway and similar marks can be found in the entrance of the church at Grinton, where the Norman archway still exists as it does here. The marks in St Oswald's however, are more plentiful and show evidence of heavy and prolonged use of the archway for this purpose.

There appears to be no historical explanation for this practice, but Yew trees have been grown in graveyards

since time immemorial, and yew wood was traditionally used for the making of arrows. Perhaps arrows made from trees growing on hallowed ground were believed to have superior powers. The Norman overlords were very fond of hunting, and these puzzling marks could have been made by servants who waited with the weapons outside, while their masters attended Mass and prayed for a successful chase.

137

Stump Cross Caverns
NIDDERDALE

Close to Pateley Bridge in Nidderdale, are the show caves of Stump Cross Caverns, a cave system carved out beneath Greenhow Hills by the action of water long ages ago.

The caves were discovered in 1858 by men who were working in the lead mines close by, and are most famous for the number of animal remains that were found. The earliest remains are of wolverine and reindeer, animals who roamed the area before the last ice age 140,000 years ago, and there were many bones of post-glacial animals; wolves, bears and deer. These remains are now in the Natural History Museum, London.

Early man did not inhabit these caves. Neolithic people generally lived in wooden houses, and although they also occupied some caves in the Dales, their main use for the many caves was as burial chambers.

Today, at Stump Cross, a quarter of a mile of the three-mile cave system is now a show cave. The damp rocks of the subterranean channels close in, and visitors must bend low to reach an impressive display of stalactites and stalagmites and some weird formations that have names such as 'The Grotto', 'Sleeping Cat', and 'The Hawk'.

Knights Templar Chapel
NEAR WEST BURTON

A long and pleasant leafy lane rises gently to the meadows and swathes of woodland which lie below the craggy limestone landmark of Dove Scar. From this height there is a truly splendid panoramic vista spreading out across Bishopdale to Wensleydale. Aysgarth church can be easily picked out and even the distant Howgill Fells can be seen on a clear day.

Near to the vantage point where Bolton Castle dominates the view, lie all that remains of a preceptory of the Knights Templar. This was a military religious order founded in Jerusalem in 1152 to protect pilgrims, and this small monastery and a hospital were built in 1200. Philip IV of France fearing the power of these religious knights instigated a violent suppression in 1312, and the order was wiped out.

In this high and unfrequented place, a cool breeze eternally sighs in the trees, carrying the sound of the curlew's lament and conjuring up a mysterious and evocative atmosphere. Half hidden in the grass rest the remains of the Templars' chapel and three open stone coffins, their small size a reminder that medieval people were much smaller in stature than we are today.

KNITTER
DENT

During the heyday of the textile and lead industries in the Dales during the 17th and 18th centuries, hand-knitting was an important way of supplementing the meagre incomes earned by miners and mill workers. Men, women and children would knit furiously as they walked to the mills, using special needles which were steadied in a wooden sheath. In the early 19th century they could earn fourpence a day, making stockings, caps and frocks.

Knitting became a major cottage industry, especially renowned for worsted stockings made from locally carded wool – all the stockings for the British army in the Napoleonic wars came from the Yorkshire Dales.

There were hand-knitting centres at Gayle and Reeth, but the craft flourished most notably to the west, in the village of Dent. Here, one individual could turn out as many as 12 woollen hats in a day, and for this prodigious output they became famously known as the 'Terrible Knitters of Dent' – 'Terrible' meaning terribly good!

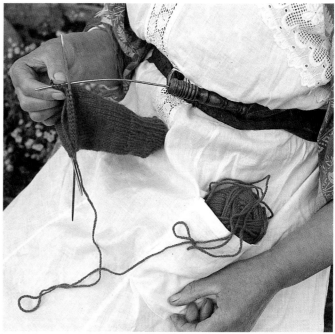

With the advent of steam power, and the change in fashion from knee breeches to long trousers, the hand-knitting industry began to decline in the last century, but it is still carried on as a local craft.

Prehistoric Settlement
INGLEBOROUGH

On the summit of Ingleborough Peak is a broad, triangular plateau where there are the scant remains of a wall and six horseshoe-shaped hut circles. Ingle means 'fire', and at over 2,300 feet, this place was perfect for ancient beacon fires. Prehistoric people would have visited here, but the lack of water would have presented a problem for any permanent settlement.

It is not certain who built this fort, but the local tribe of Brigantes may have made a stand against the Roman invaders from here. The wall could be attributed to the Romans, for after they had captured the summit they would certainly have made use of its high vantage point.

In 1830 a tower was built here, intended as a hospice, or shelter for those who clambered to this wind-blown place, and unfortunately some of the stones from the ancient fort were used in its construction. Only a heap of rubble remains on the site now, for the tower was destroyed by drunken workmen as soon as it was finished.

Gunnerside Gill
SWALEDALE

Here, looking down snow-covered Gunnerside Gill, the man-made scars and ruins on the hillside are hidden from view, and this could be any part of Swaledale. But the melting snow will reveal all the evidence of the lead mining that once went on here in the famous Old Gang mining complex. During the heydays of lead mining, many farmers would spend the winter months as miners, and return to the land in the summer.

The stream rises about six miles away below Rogan's Seat, and Gunnerside village, with its cottages built up the hillside, can be seen at its foot. A typical linear Dales village, new dwellings were built between existing houses during the 19th century, and this has resulted in a long unbroken line of architecture. It is the largest village in the dale and gets its name from the Anglo/Viking name of a local chieftain; the name means 'Gunnar's pasture'. The Yorkshire writer Thomas Armstrong lived nearby, and set his novel *Adam Brunskill* in this lead-mining community, describing in vivid detail the hardship of life here during the last century.

Inscribed Lintel
HAWES

George Fox was the son of a Leicestershire weaver, and when he became disenchanted with the established church he set out on a journey across the land to seek spiritual guidance. It was in the Yorkshire Dales, on Pendle Hill in Ribblesdale, that he had a vision of hundreds of people, clad in white, assembling by a river. He began to preach his message of simple Christianity, and the people who flocked to hear his stirring oratory, found that the Society of Friends were determined to act on their beliefs.

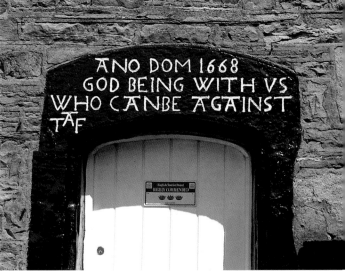

The wealthier Quakers (so nicknamed because they were said to quake before God) were great benefactors and helped the struggling poor of the region in many ways. In 1792 Robert Foster built Hebblethwaite Hall Woollen Mill, and established a school to provide employment and education for the poor. Later, Quakers established the London Lead Company, and took over the mines at Marrick and Grinton, leasing others elsewhere. They improved the conditions for many mineworkers.

Thomas Fawcett was an early Quaker who built his house in the old cattle market in Hawes in 1668. It is now a hotel, but the words that he had inscribed over the doorway have been preserved.

Wesleyan Methodist Chapel

CAUTLEY NEAR SEDBERGH

In the 18th century, John Wesley came to the north, driven away from the established church. Forbidden to preach his message of strict religious discipline in the churches, he was forced to broadcast his message by preaching in the open.

He found many willing listeners in the Yorkshire Dales' lead-mining areas, for the people had been largely neglected by the Anglican church, and these were a tough and unfanciful people, used to hardship.

Travelling preachers would be sent out to the remotest areas, and Cautley, in the shadow of the Howgill Fells must have been a lonely place in those days. Many such meeting places for worship sprang up, even in the tiniest hamlets, and by 1851 the Wesleyan circuit based in Reeth recorded an average Sunday attendance of 1,400.

However, with the closing of the lead mines the people moved away and Methodism suffered a swift decline, but its chapels are still to be found in every corner of the Dales.

Preston's Folly
SETTLE

The interesting doorway of Preston's Folly is just part of an attractive and intriguing building which was constructed on the outskirts of Settle in about 1675.

Richard Preston was a wealthy mercer and local landowner who had the building constructed as a gentleman's residence in a highly idiosyncratic style. He called it Tanner's Hall which may hint at the original source of his wealth, but it has long been more familiarly known as Preston's Folly. It was situated on the old main road to Settle and its odd mixture of styles, combining what was then very modern, with older and more traditional features, made it a great focus of interest.

Its external appearance is Tudor, and the windows of the upper storeys are very plain, but those on the ground floor are quite different, and run the length of the walls on either side of the main doorway, extending around the corners. These corners, which lack supporting quoins, were regarded as a weakness in the structure, and it was thought that they would lead to the ruination of the house.

However this fine old building still stands, and will continue to do so for many years to come.

Winter Fuel
HALTON GILL

Piles of wood are seen here stacked for use as fuel in the Dales' most isolated hamlet of Halton Gill.

When wood was plentiful in the valleys, the village populations were often granted the right to coppice the trees and gather firewood, and villagers who lived close to the moors had rights of 'turbary', which meant that the peat could be dug freely, but it was hard work to cut enough fuel to last throughout the winter.

Coal has been used throughout the Dales for hundreds of years, for there were many mines to be found on the hills, and the seams were usually close to the surface. This easily obtained fuel has been mined since the 13th and 14th centuries, when coal from Tan Hill was used at the great monasteries and castles. In 1384 a quarter of a ton of coal cost tenpence.

Coal was mined most heavily during the 18th and 19th centuries when, aside from its domestic use it was needed to fire the lead-smelting mills, and the lime kilns. However, when the new railway began to transport cheaper coal from Durham, the mines of the dales were deserted.

Old Gang Lead Mine
NEAR REETH

The ruins of the lead mines of the Dales have an almost unearthly atmosphere, and the man-made scars and scratches on the hillsides add a melancholy beauty that contrasts with, but does not detract from, the loveliness of the surrounding landscape. Here the long defunct Old Gang mines near Reeth draw many visitors.

The Romans were the first to exploit the mineral, using the local tribe of Brigantes as slaves to work the mines. The richest source of lead was found in Swaledale.

Lead is found in veins, and some 'ore shoots' could be half a mile long and as much as 100 feet deep. In Swaledale most of the veins were reached by adits dug straight into the hillside, and by 'hushing': water from streams higher up was held back and then allowed to rush over the opened veins, washing the mineral out and down the hillside. Evidence of 'hushes' can be seen everywhere.

Half a million tons of lead were obtained from Swaledale, but by the end of the last century the price of the mineral had plummeted. Everywhere the noise and bustle of the work was halted, and an eerie silence reigned.

C.B. Inn
ARKENGARTHDALE

The C.B. Inn is one of the hundreds of inns and alehouses which littered the Dales in the past. Many of the hostelries had their origins in the middle ages when there was a continual movement of people travelling the length and breadth of this land. Charles Bathurst, who was the owner of the lead-mining area of Arkengarthdale, gave this pub his initials.

The men who trod the packhorse trails used regular stopping places, and the hard-working drovers' enthusiasm for relaxation and refreshment led to frequent drunken brawls at their chosen inns. Until the 1830 Beerhouse Act, any householder was permitted to sell beer but as there was a tremendous demand, the public houses flourished alongside these private outlets. The 1851 census records 22 innkeepers in Swaledale and only the Temperance Movement had any effect on the prodigious levels of beer consumed. Many public houses, like the C.B. Inn, were used by local miners, and the Methodists tried to exert a great influence on the profligacy of these poor men who led such hard and dangerous lives.

Today inns such as this can still be found in peaceful, sometimes now-deserted places, offering warm hospitality to the traveller as they have done for centuries.

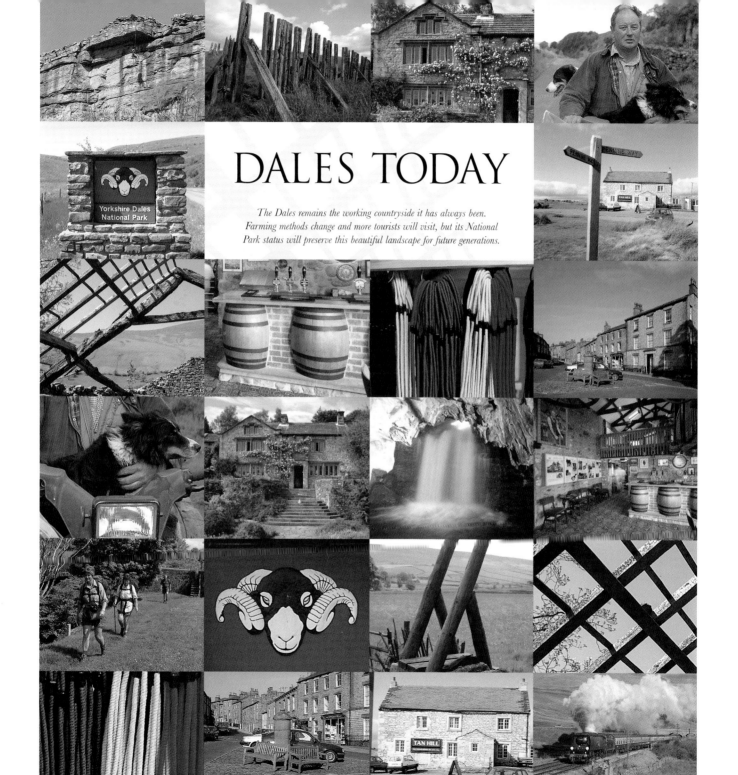

DALES TODAY

The Dales remains the working countryside it has always been. Farming methods change and more tourists will visit, but its National Park status will preserve this beautiful landscape for future generations.

Rock Climbing
MALHAM

The many crags and cliffs of this landscape are a magnet for those people who relish the thrill of inching their way up to some breathtaking vantage point while others keep to the safety of pathways or, as here at Malham, a well-built stairway.

Kilnsey Crag in Wharfedale is not as high as this one, but it does have a 40-feet overhang which makes it a popular venue for climbers, and from the road, abseilers can often be seen bouncing down its sides.

The sheer face of the cliff at Malham Cove has long been irresistible to climbers, and there are several well-used routes along the thin cracks which run up its smooth, exposed face; when they have conquered this, there is another more challenging climb at the other end of the village. Here the sheer and impressive walls of Gordale Scar offer a wonderful sense of achievement to the experienced climbing enthusiast, as well as some alarming entertainment for those who watch from the reassuringly solid ground below.

Theakstons and Masham
MASHAM

The brewery at Masham has provided the public houses of the Yorkshire Dales with beer for generations; the most popular and best known is 'Old Peculier'. The brewery has become a place of pilgrimage, for this beer is one of Yorkshire's oldest brews, taking it's name from 'Peculier', the medieval official whose modern day counterpart would be responsible for weights and measures.

The brewery has been here since 1827, near to Masham's enormous market square, where there was once a bull ring and set of stocks. A market has been held here since 1250 and Masham was granted its official charter in 1393, by Stephen le Scrope. Today, there is still a popular weekly market, although the town has declined in importance during this century.

Masham's church has many Victorian additions and improvements but it was originally Norman. Much of the 11th-century interior remains, and the tower survives, surmounted by a tall spire. In the churchyard stands an impressive ancient stone column, that dates back to the 7th century. It is decorated with representations of the 12 apostles and a depiction of the 'Adoration of the Magi'.

Parceval Hall
NEAR APPLETREEWICK

Set on a hillside close to the village of Appletreewick, Parceval Hall commands wonderful views over Wharfedale. It was originally a late Tudor farmhouse, and still retains some of its original features. The hall now belongs to the centre of pilgrimage at Walsingham, and is used by the diocese of Bradford as a centre for retreats and conferences.

The architect Sir William Milner was enchanted by the Hall and its superb position when he first saw it in the early 1920s. When he had bought it, he had it restored, adding new wings using old stones from nearby derelict buildings. This sympathetic restoration resulted in a house of exquisite charm, rendered quite picturesque by the surrounding shrubs and climbing roses. There is a chapel in the house, dedicated to Our Lady of Walsingham. It is so small that there was only enough room for the priest, Sir William, and his dog.

The gardens are open to the public and in the grounds are beautiful walks, winding through woodland and past streams, pools and rock gardens.

Sheep Farmer and Dogs
SWALEDALE

In most of the Dales, particularly in the upper reaches, the only farming that has ever been possible is sheep farming, and many people here are carrying on the traditional way of life that their forbears have done for many hundreds of years.

Farmers today obtain permits to graze their animals on the high common land, each sheep and its progeny counting as one 'gait'. The number of sheep is strictly controlled and farmers are allowed only a certain number of gaits.

Most of the fells and moorland is unenclosed and the sheep apparently wander unrestricted. However, this freedom to roam is checked somewhat by the sheep's inbred sense of place. This is known as being 'heufed', and because of this the farmers task of rounding up his flocks is not as difficult as might be imagined. Modern shepherds can rely on trail bikes or land buggies to move around these areas.

Today as in the past, though, sheep farming in the Dales would be impossible without the irreplaceable sheepdog. The Swaledale sheep have a strong and wilful character and they graze far and wide over very rough terrain, so his dogs are as vital to this modern shepherd as his motorbike.

Dales Way
DENTDALE

The Yorkshire Dales is criss-crossed by a network of paths, many of which sprang into being back in the mists of time, when Neolithic people first settled here with their tough little sheep and cattle. There are the narrow footpaths leading from one hamlet to another, many worn by churchgoers down the ages, as they walked to Sunday services at the distant 'Mother' churches. Wide drove-roads run for miles; these once linked the monasteries with the far-flung Granges where their sheep were tended. There are also the old packhorse roads used to transport goods in and out of this remote region. People come now to follow some of the 1,100 miles of tracks within the Yorkshire Dales National Park, and many of the waymarked, official routes follow the ancient pathways.

The first long-distance path, and the most impressive, is the Pennine Way which traverses some rough and challenging terrain, but those who tread the Dales Way Long Distance Path will find it less rigorous, and with its wonderful variety of scenery, it is claimed by some to be much more enjoyable.

Derelict Barn
BISHOPDALE

The rafters of this decaying field barn show starkly against the sky; sad evidence that life in the Yorkshire Dales is changing, and with it the landscape. These familiar rectangular stone buildings, nestling against the stone-walled enclosures, have been an integral feature of this countryside for generations, but modern farming practices are now making them redundant.

Farmers no longer store the hay for winter feed in these scattered barns. Their cattle, who were once sheltered in them, now spend the long winter months in huge central sheds, close to the farmhouse. Increasingly, they are fed on silage which does not need to be stored in the barns. This is sound farming practice economically, but aesthetically unattractive.

As they fall into disuse, many of these old barns are allowed to deteriorate by the farmers who cannot afford to preserve them. Tourism, however, may be the saving of them. As there are volunteers rebuilding neglected stone walls within the National Park, so there are moves to preserve these lovely historical old buildings for future generations to enjoy.

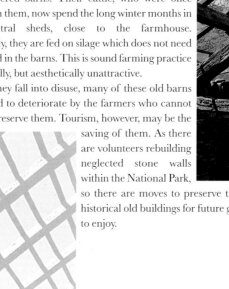

Settle to Carlisle Railway
RIBBLESDALE

Trailing a magnificent head of steam, the 'City of Wells' train flies along the moorland tracks of the Settle to Carlisle Railway.

The coming of the railways to the Yorkshire Dales began in the 1850s and the Settle to Carlisle line was opened in 1876. The building of this railway across such territory was fraught with dangers. Beyond the Ribblehead viaduct, Blea Moor spreads northwards and presented great problems for the men who forced the tunnel through the rock. The navvies suffered unimaginable hardship and danger, for constant dynamiting and drilling was necessary to excavate the hard gritstone and limestone.

The Blea Moor tunnel reaches a depth of 500 feet and is 3,000 yards long, emerging on Dentdale. Completed in 1875 it cost hundreds of lives, and there is a memorial to these men in the little chapel at Chapel-le-Dale. The construction workers and navvies inhabited shanty towns such as the one at Batty Moss, where the hard working men would spend their evenings in the taverns, drinking and carousing, and earning themselves great notoriety.

Today, steam trains such as this are still in use, carrying their passengers through some of the country's most beautiful and most inaccessible countryside.

Rope Works
HAWES

Brightly coloured lengths of rope make for an eye-catching display in the rope-making visitor centre at Hawes. This local industry has been established at Gate House since 1922, but the history of the craft in this village goes back more than 200 years, and today the rope works can be seen in action, spinning and whirling hypnotically as the yarns are twisted into various thicknesses.

This modern rope works now specialises in ropes for church bells, barriers, animal halters and dog leads, but years ago rope was needed for many other purposes, and had to be twisted by hand.

One of the most important tools for the farmers of the Dales was the hay creel and many were produced here. The creel consisted of two slim sticks which were bent into a 'D' shape. Thin rope was then attached in a wide mesh joining the two shapes. Hay could then be carried to the animals in the hammock-shaped creel.

Creels are no longer needed but sheep 'hopples' can still be useful. These are soft, wide pieces of cotton webbing which can be attached diagonally to a sheep's legs, and are sometimes used to restrain any adventurous animal bent on scaling the stone walls.

Park Sign
YORKSHIRE DALES NATIONAL PARK

The likeness of a Swaledale ram can be seen everywhere on signs within the Yorkshire Dales National Park.

After the passing of the National Parks Act of 1949, ten National Parks were established. They included 680 square miles of the Yorkshire Dales, although the traditional Dales boundaries cover a much larger area. The objective was to 'preserve and enhance the natural beauty of the area and to promote opportunities for outdoor recreation' and the National Parks Authority is responsible for maintaining paths and giving information. In the Yorkshire Dales they fulfil this purpose admirably, providing advice and assistance to the many visitors who come to indulge in caving, pot-holing and climbing, or simply walking the miles of footpaths and reveling in the breathtaking scenery.

However the Dales truly belong to the people whose families have lived and worked here for generations, and the National Parks Authority has a policy which gives highest priority to their interests. Without the people, the Park would be a poorer place, and a country code ensures that all who wander here treat this special area with proper respect.

Skeldale House
ASKRIGG

Askrigg is a small village of 17th- and 18th-century, gritstone houses, which have a more elegant and prosperous aspect than the homely cottages of other Dales villages.

It developed as a trading village on the edge of the forest, later becoming a famed clock-making centre, and until the late 18th century it was the most important village in Upper Wensleydale. Where the main road widens, near the 16th-century church, there is a cobbled area with a cross and bull ring, and behind the church a footpath leads to two waterfalls: Mill Gill and Whitfield Gill tumbling down a steep wooded ravine.

This is a pleasant and interesting village, but its great popularity with visitors lies in its location as the fictional Darrowby of the television series *All Creatures Great and Small*. The real James Herriot was called Alf Wight and he worked from Thirsk, but Askrigg was considered a better location, and Skeldale House will be instantly recognised by followers of the series as Herriot's veterinary surgery.

Tan Hill Pub
TAN HILL

Tan Hill rises to 1,732 feet, and even in summer, cool winds can sweep across the rock-strewn heather and grass. Roads from Keld, Arkengarthdale and Brough meet on these heights, and all about on the bleak moorland, shallow depressions mark the positions of the bell-shaped pits of the old mining excavations.

'Tan' means 'fire' in Celtic, and this probably links the hill with their Beltane beacon fires, and very early coal mining here. The earliest known records date from 1296, and Lady Anne Clifford is known to have used Tan Hill coal when staying at Appleby. The mining of coal is inextricably linked to the great Dales lead mining era of the 18th and 19th centuries as it was essential for smelting.

Life for the people who lived on this cold, desolate hill must have been unimaginably hard, not least for the children who went to school down in Keld, four miles away.

Tan Hill is the highest pub in England, and stands by the Pennine Way, offering welcome shelter to hardy walkers. In 1974 boundary changes put the pub in County Durham, but vociferous opposition by the people of Yorkshire ensured that the boundary was moved.

Stile Over Stone Wall
HORTON-IN-RIBBLESDALE

The public footpaths of the Dales generally take the walker by the shortest route from place to place, crossing land which is mainly still privately owned. Before the enclosure acts there was not much need for stiles, but the high stone walls which now enmesh the hills and dales, are as effective at restricting human, as well as animal wanderlust.

Where the walls cut across a well-used pathway, the wallers incorporated a sheep-proof stile. The most common is a high narrow gap, reached by steps built into the stonework, but along the paths leading from the villages to the nearest church, a complete gap has been left. Made too narrow for sheep to pass through, often by the use of flagstones to make a 'V' shaped gap, they would have accommodated the long skirts and 'Sunday Best' clothes of the churchgoers. On the field path from Aysgarth village to the church, some rather unusual and attractive rounded pillars have been used at the stiles, and their smooth surfaces make squeezing through the stile much easier even today.

High ladder stiles such as this one are an innovation of the age of tourism, ensuring that walls remain undamaged. They also provide splendid high vantage points from which to survey the landscape.

White Scar Cave
INGLEBOROUGH

There was a time, when visitors first came to see the spectacular features of this limestone country-side, that it almost became known as the Cave District. Here, where pot-holes swallow streams, and water percolates through the rock, there are many caves which mark the reappearance of underground rivers, and White Scar Cave is, for many, the most impressive of these.

At Ingleborough's foot, and close to the village of Chapel-le-Dale, White Scar was discovered in 1923 by Christopher Long. The cave was carved out by the resurgence of water from Crina Bottom and Boggarts Roaring Holes.

The original entrance was very low; it has since been enlarged to turn it into a magnificent show cave, and there are over 400 yards of paths which hundreds of visitors follow every year. Lights shine on the myriad stalactites bristling from the roofs of the caverns, and the glistening stalagmites, subterranean streams and thundering waterfalls.

Snow Fence
DENT STATION

The winters in the Dales are long and bitter, especially so in the higher areas where great drifts of snow can isolate farms and villages for weeks. Dent station is the highest in England, so this fence has been placed as a barrier to prevent the sudden avalanches that could smother the lines of the Settle to Carlisle railway.

The Dales has its own micro-climate, and the changeable nature of the weather plays a great part in the splendour of the scenery. Rain can fall heavily, but frequently passes on in minutes leaving an exhilarating sparkle in the air, and cloud shadows flickering over the hills and dales.

In winter the snow lends the craggy landscape a magical and unearthly beauty. Spring comes late, and with it the new lambs and spring flowers and everywhere the sound of rushing streams and waterfalls, icy with meltwater. Summer brings the glories of the wildflowers and purple moors, and when the sun beats down the limestone dazzles, and the cool green shade of the woods are a haven.

As summer wanes, the slanting light of the sun throws the stone walls and barns into sharp relief and lights up the leaves and bracken with the colours of fire.

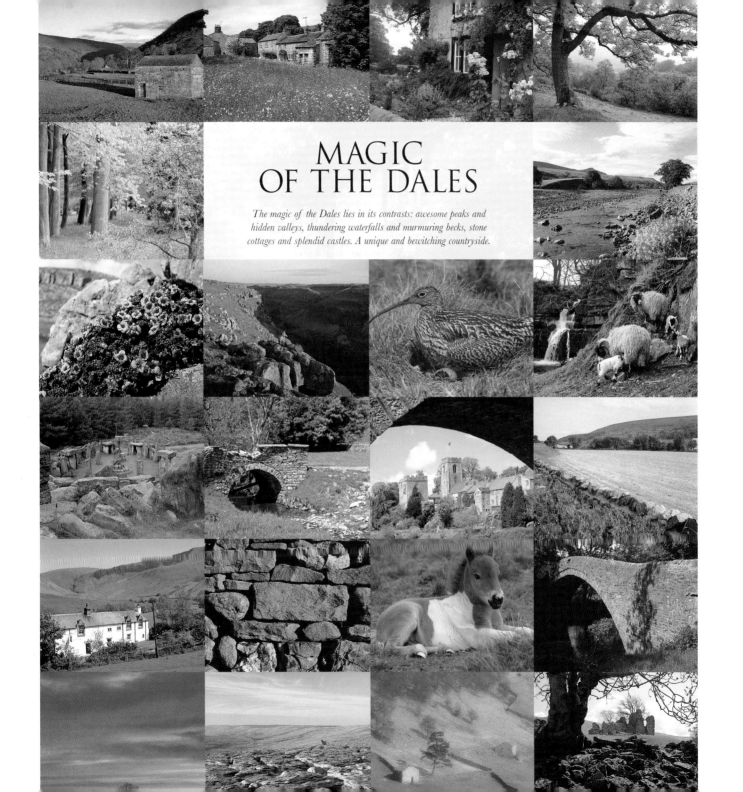

MAGIC
OF THE DALES

The magic of the Dales lies in its contrasts: awesome peaks and hidden valleys, thundering waterfalls and murmuring becks, stone cottages and splendid castles. A unique and bewitching countryside.

Thorpe Perrow Arboretum
NEAR BEDALE

Pink blossom froths above an infinite carpet of bluebells, one of the abundant delights of spring-time in Thorpe Perrow Arboretum near Bedale.

In 1927 Colonel Sir Leonard Ropner was given 85 acres of the family's parkland by his father. Some of the ancient oak trees on this land had been growing since the time of Henry VIII, and Sir Leonard, fired with enthusiasm, began to plant an outstanding collection of trees and plants.

He brought hundreds of specimens back from forays all over the world, and planted them in a delightfully naturalistic display of woodland and gardens. This deliberate 'artlessness' has all the appearance of a perfectly wild woodland, albeit planted with rare species.

The Arboretum took 50 years to complete, and has now been extended to include a 16th-century Spring Wood, with each specimen carefully labelled for added interest. Sir John Ropner manages the collection now, which consists of over 2,000 species of trees and shrubs, including more than 60 varieties of lilac.

Swaledale Sheep
SWALEDALE

The sound of sheep calling has echoed around the Dales for thousands of years, and they have played a large part in the shaping of the landscape since Neolithic men brought their flocks here to graze. The well-drained country meant that the animals were less prone to foot-rot, and it is probably due to the over-grazing of these early flocks that we have the bare limestone plateaux of today.

Sheep farming has long been the mainstay of the economy here, and during 400 years of monastic power, and its dependency on the wool trade, the wide sheep walks sprang up. Sheep are nimble climbers, and this dictated the altitude of one of the most characteristic features of the Dales – the miles of stone walls. The legion watercourses of the land, powered the woollen mills of later years, providing the wealth to build grand houses.

Arable crops will not grow in much of this region, and down the ages, Dalespeople have relied on the ability of their hardy breeds of sheep, such as these Swaledales, to cope with the long bitter winters. In contrast, cattle would perish in the Dales weather without protection.

There could be no better emblem for the Yorkshire Dales than a sheep.

Cross Keys Inn
CAUTLEY

Buzzards circle above the steep and narrow valley which rises up behind the whitewashed Cross Keys Inn. Set against the green backdrop of the close-looming humps of the Howgill Fells, the inn was built in 1732, and must have been a welcome sight to those who travelled along the lonely road from Sedbergh.

Here on the western fringes of the Yorkshire Dales, the landscape differs noticeably from the wide valleys and craggy tops which characterise the dales to the east, for these hills lie on the border of the Lake District where the ice was exceptionally thick during the last Ice Age. This high mass of ice moved very slowly over the mountain tops without the scraping and smoothing effects of the glaciers on the eastern side, leaving rounded hills and narrow clefts where villages could never become established. However, a small glacier did form in the hollow on this eastern side of the fell, scouring and enlarging it. Soil and debris tumbled down and filled it so that now, in a fold of the hills behind the inn, a spectacular waterfall drops 1,000 feet beside the dark and awesome Cautley Crag.

Curlew
SLEDDALE

If the black-faced Swaledale ram were to be replaced by another symbol of the Yorkshire Dales National Park there would be two contenders for his place: the red grouse and the curlew.

The red grouse is unique to Britain and inhabits the moorland where it feeds on ling heather. It is a shy and secretive bird, and is most likely to appear suddenly when startled, its chunky body carried away on whirring wings, and its croaking call, 'go-bak, go-bak', is familiar to all who roam its habitat. Other birds leave to find milder climates when summer wanes, but the hardy grouse stoically remains on the moors and braves the worst of the winter, when it will tread the snow with its feathered feet to avoid being buried.

The curlew is a secretive bird too, especially when nesting, but it can be seen in spring, gliding and spiralling down to claim nesting territories on the moors. Once only found on moorland, it can now be found almost anywhere in Britain However, It is this bird's melancholy call, so redolent of the loneliest reaches of this awe inspiring landscape, that links it inextricably with the Yorkshire Dales.

Tree near Cray
WHARFEDALE

This delightful scene can be enjoyed in the peace and seclusion of the upper reaches of Wharfedale, where the little farming hamlet of Cray sits on a ridge above Crook Gill.

The small valley here is full of the species of trees and plants that covered these hills before the last Ice Age. The glacier which carved Wharfedale's wide 'U' shape also swept away the trees and the soil too, so that even after 10,000 years the trees have never been re-established on the high ground to the west of Cray. A few woodland plants can be seen there, sheltering in the fissures of a platform of limestone pave-

ments, but the ice floe moved directly south, passing this little side valley by, so it escaped the worst of the glacial damage.

It is a truly idyllic place, where trees overhang small waterfalls and a hurrying stream where fossils can be found. There is a small packhorse bridge here, and the people who once passed this way would have looked upon the same delightful scenery for many centuries.

Field Barn
SWALEDALE

The many solid barns which dot the valleys and hillsides have become an integral feature of the landscape and were once a vital part of pastoral farming in the Yorkshire Dales.

Made of the same local stone as the enclosure walls, they blend harmoniously and add a special charm to the scenery. Indeed, the multitude of barns which are gathered in Upper Swaledale below Buttertubs Pass, are one of the area's most photographed sights.

These barns have two floors; the lower part housed the stock during the long winters lasting from November to May, and the hay would be stored in the loft above. The hay had to be grown and harvested by the end of July, and a poor summer could have a disastrous effect on supplies of this essential fodder.

The barn sizes differ from dale to dale and so do the names. They are called variously: laithes, cow-houses, field-houses, shippons, and mistrals, and the small barns are hogg houses, built to provide shelter for the early lambs, known as hoggs. There are also small stone buildings to be found on the remote and unpopulated fells and moors, and these are the bothies which gave shelter to the shepherds at lambing time.

Marmion Tower
WEST TANFIELD

Along the bridge Lord Marmion rode,
Proudly his red-roan charger trode,
His helm hung at the saddlebow;
Well by his visage you might know
He was a stalworth knight, and keen...

Sir Walter Scott 'Marmion'.

In the eastern Dales between Masham and Ripon, the delightful village of West Tanfield stands quietly overlooking the River Ure as it meanders southwards.

The village is dominated by an impressive Tudor gate house with a beautiful oriel window. This is Marmion Tower which is all that remains of the manor house which once belonged to the Marmion family. They have all vanished along with their ancestral home, but their effigies lie with their tombs in the 14th-century church. The tower remains much as it would have been when it belonged to Elizabeth Parr, the grandmother of Katherine.

The tower inspired Sir Walter Scott's narrative poem 'Marmion' with its romantic hero, the young highlander Lochinvar. Written in 1808 it is set in the time of Henry VIII, and tells how Lord Marmion spurns the Lady Constance in pursuit of the wealthy Lady Clare. Ultimately Marmion meets his end at the battle of Flodden Field. Disappointingly however, it appears that no Marmion was actually at Flodden.

Wild Boar Fell and Mallerstang
NEAR MALLERSTANG EDGE

Wild Boar Fell is said to be the place where the last Wild Boar in the Dales was killed by Sir Richard Musgrave in the fifteenth century. There could well be some substance to the story as his tomb was opened when the Kirkby Stephen Chapel was being restored, and a boar's tusk was found to be buried with him.

The fearsome beauty of Wild Boar Fell and High Seat rise above the line of crags at Mallerstang Edge, to more than 2,000 feet. From Wild Boar Fell there are stupendous views as far as the Lake District to the west, and over Swaledale to the east. This is the watershed for rivers that flow into the Irish Sea and for the Swale and Ure which run through the Dales to the North Sea.

Below Wild Boar Fell is Hell Gill Force, where the Ure drops into a nightmare chasm. There is now a bridge here but a legend says that Dick Turpin fled this way whilst being pursued by the law. Black Bess is reputed to have leapt the chasm, carrying Turpin out of the clutches of his pursuers. Locals insist that the daring highwayman was one of their own.

Constable Burton Hall
NEAR LEYBURN

The Georgian elegance of Constable Burton Hall near Leyburn, was designed by John Carr. Built in 1768 for Sir Marmaduke Wyvill, it is still occupied by the Wyvill family. They have opened the delightful gardens to the public, who can wander through woodland and terraces, filled with a wonderful kaleidoscope of colour, ever changing with the seasons.

Here, dappled sunlight falls on one of the pretty borders of summer flowers, and everywhere there is a feast for the eyes. There are fragile cyclamen and alpine plants, and the great loops of the rope-like stems of 'Old Man's Beard', hanging from tall conifers. There are lilies and magnolia trees, and the many varieties of acer glow with colour. In spring, a splendid show of daffodils carpets the ground beneath a group of majestic oak trees. A pathway leads through a cool avenue of limes, and by a lightly wooded stream to a pretty lily pond.

The fine botanical specimens, planted with subtle and artistic flair, rather than stiff formality, make these gardens a joy. The river flows below the gardens to the rear of the house, and it overlooks spreading parkland where cattle graze, adding to the timeless air of tranquillity which surrounds it.

Ivelet Bridge
SWALEDALE

The pretty Ghyll dale of Oxnop is full of the chatter of little waterfalls, and the trees and shrubs that once covered much of Swaledale before the land was cleared for pasture. Mountain ash, hawthorn, holly and willow grow thickly, and made a favourite haunt for the famous Victorian naturalists Richard and Cherry Kearton, who lived in the valley below.

To reach this little wildlife paradise they would certainly have used the old footpath

which leads down to the floor of Swaledale to cross river at Ivelet. Here there is a high, single-arched packhorse bridge that must surely be the most attractive in the Dales. This is part of the old Corpse Way, and long ago, the deceased of remote areas had to be carried across the river to be taken on to the hallowed ground at Grinton church. These days cars can cross the bridge, although the pronounced hump could cause trouble for some with low suspension.

Ivelet Bridge is also apparently haunted by a headless black dog – a portentous creature of ill omen – which disappears on passing over the bridge.

Village Green
ARNCLIFFE

The village of Arncliffe in beautiful Littondale is noted for its flower-filled green and is a justifiable source of local pride. In the Dales there are many villages such as this, which have grown up around a green or market square. This cluster pattern had its origins in the times when the fierce bands of Scots marauders came on cattle-stealing raids, for stock could be quickly driven onto the green, where they would be better protected.

The paved market squares are generally confined to the larger villages and towns such as Leyburn and Masham, which have held market charters for centuries. Fairs and livestock markets were held on these paved squares where old bull rings can still be seen – bull-baiting was once a widespread entertainment. Some villages still display a set of stocks on their greens which also undoubtedly provided their own questionable entertainment.

The smaller village greens such as this one, continue to be a focal point for local communities. Fêtes are held on them, and Morris dancers perform there, entertaining the local people as the travelling thespians and mummers of the past once did their ancestors.

Stone Wall
SWALEDALE

Although some ancient walled enclosures date from the days when the monasteries grazed their sheep here, but the familiar spectacle of numberless stone walls reaching across the Dales today, appeared only about a hundred years ago.

A series of Parliamentary Enclosure Acts resulted in their construction over a period of just 50 years. During this time, hundreds of men built most of this tremendous network of walls – the surname Waller is still common here. They used carefully chosen stones and worked to precise specifications. The double-skinned walls, five to six feet high, have a base of three feet, narrowing to 18 inches at the top. The two parallel walls would be built up with the local limestone or sandstone rocks and boulders. Small rocks and pebbles filled in the spaces, and the Enclosure Act insisted that at each rood (seven feet) large flat stones or 'stretchers' should be laid to render the walls more stable.

These endless miles of straight stone walls which criss-cross the Dales, prevent the sheep from wandering and provide shelter. Sturdy and windproof they protect the animals from the worst of the harsh weather which can grip the dales, and offer cool shade under a hot summer sun.

Field Bridge
CAUTLEY

At Cautley, water radiates down from both sides of the valley, and the many streams and becks babble through the fields to join the River Rawthey. In this quiet and overlooked part of the Dales an attractive arched bridge presents a delightful picture.

Bridges of every size cross the numerous rivers and streams of this water-filled countryside. The very ancient clapper bridges are simply slabs of stone which reach from bank to bank, being supported by rocks mid-stream, and have been used since time immemorial. Low-sided packhorse bridges were situated on the main routes through the Dales, for sure-footed ponies were once the only way of transporting goods over the rough terrain, and quietly placed bridges such as this would have seen much use before the advent of modern roads and transport.

The grandest bridges were built with the wealth generated by the lead mining and textile industries of the 17th and 10th centuries, and are confined to the 'civilised' eastern towns such as Richmond and Ripon. However, this charming and modest little bridge still stands as an example of the wealth of pleasant surprises that lie in so many unfrequented corners of the Dales.

Stone Cottage
RIBBLESDALE

Roses thrive in the Dales. The arching branches of the wild rose display their delicate pink blooms in all the valleys, here their cultivated cousins clamber over a Ribblesdale cottage, softening the grey stone.

Throughout the Yorkshire Dales, the summer visitor can delight in the neat uniformity of the mellow stone houses, and walled gardens. Whether the villages are clustered around a green, or strung out alongside the road, they blend harmoniously with the backdrop of sparkling white scars and green hillsides, and although they lack 'chocolate box' glamour, they are still a pleasure to behold.

The local stone and simplicity of the houses are a perfect foil for the flower gardens; pansies and petunias mingle with foxgloves and daisies, echoing the floral displays of the fields and verges. Sometimes limewash brightens the stones, but Dalespeople rely on their gardens for colour, tending them with pride, and an unkempt front garden is a rarity. Everywhere, flowers tumble in an artless profusion which belies the cold winters, and this lovely show is surely one of the most pleasurable sights that the Dales has to offer.

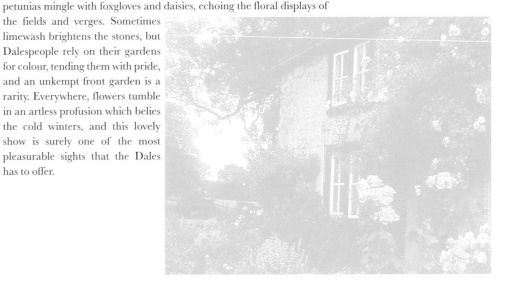

Moorland Pony
NEAR GARSDALE

This delightful little foal is one of the tough breed of mountain ponies who roam much of the unenclosed moorland of the western dales, and these wild fell ponies were undoubtedly the ancestors of the 'Dales pony'.

For many years this strong and reliable breed was the mainstay of life in the Dales, where the farmers called it 't'Dales Gallowa'. It was an even-tempered and willing utility pony, widely used as a packhorse and in the shafts. These ponies were strong enough to carry lead and coal from the mines, as well as shepherds and hay to the flocks who grazed the fells.

Their ability to withstand the bitter winters of the northern Dales and to thrive on poor grassland was legendary, and the ponies were generally regarded with great affection by their owners.

With the coming of petrol-driven mowing machines and tractors the ponies vanished from the landscape, but in 1916 The Dales Pony Society was established and today there is a renewed interest in this historic breed.

Fox On A Crag
ABOVE MALHAM

Perched on a high limestone crag, a fox catches the first rays of sunlight and surveys his world. He has probably been enticed by the presence of rabbits who thrive on the poor vegetation about the rocky outcrops and pavements, for they are the only companions of the sheep who graze here.

Foxes will generally be found where hunting is easier, and most of the animals in the Dales inhabit the lower altitudes where the climate is more benign and the plant life more abundant. Deer inhabit the scar woods and the old hunting forests, and there are red squirrels to be found

in the wooded ravines at Ingleton, but the greatest variety of creatures are found where there is the greatest variety of plants and trees: the meadowland and hedgerows of the valley floors. In summer the meadows hum with the sound of a multitude of insects and there is an abundance of familiar animals. Stoats and weasels, hedgehogs, field mice and voles, all flourish here, and bats find ideal homes in the barns, all playing their part in the cycle of life in the Dales.

Wildflowers
NEAR REETH

Poppies make vivid scarlet splashes amongst a multitude of wildflowers bordering a hay meadow in Swaledale.

The hay meadows have long been an essential part of farming in the Dales, providing winter feed for the animals who are sheltered in low fields and barns during the winter months. The flat valley floors are unsuitable for any kind of arable farming, and for centuries these riverside pastures have produced sweet hay with their abundance of wildflowers and grasses.

Sadly, these are now in decline, for farming in the uncertain climate of Dales is hard, and more economic ways of producing winter feed are being widely used; silage is made, harvesting the meadows before the wildflowers can set and disperse their seeds. Chemical fertilisers are used, doubling the hay yield of naturally manured land, but at the expense of many precious wildflowers.

However, the old traditional methods are still used by some farmers, and flowers such as the wild orchids and cowslips can still be found. Some of the most beautiful meadows of all belong to Swaledale where The Yorkshire Wildlife Trust has bought 'Yellands Meadow', and under its protection three acres of wildflowers are allowed to grow in wonderful profusion.

Ilton Stonehenge
NEAR MASHAM

In a small clearing of the forest, apparently ancient stones form an elliptical circle, surrounding a central 'altar'. They bear a striking similarity to the great circle at Stonehenge. This is not an ancient temple, however but a very unusual folly.

William Danby of Swinton Park, built his 'Druids Temple' in 1820 when the building of follies was very fashionable. They became status symbols, with various landowners attempting to upstage their neighbours, some even employing 'hermits' to inhabit the 'ruins' which they had built.

William Danby's neighbour owned the lovely formal gardens at Studeley Royal and the romantic and genuine ruin of Fountains Abbey; this inspired Danby's idea for a Druid's Temple. He was also a philanthropic man, given to charitable works, and he was pleased to give employment to the local people with the building of his folly.

The temple originally stood alone, but now the dark wood has moved in to enclose it, lending an air of mystery which would have pleased Mr Danby.

Autumn
KISDON HILL

The bracken-covered slopes of Kisdon Hill glow like gold in the autumn sunlight, which lights up the old stone barns and walls that are such a feature of Swaledale.

Kisdon means 'Little Hill' in Celtic, but this is certainly a misnomer, as it rises to over 1,600 feet, dominating the head of Swaledale. The Swale once flowed to the west of Kisdon Hill, but as a result of a glacial dam near Thwaite, its course was diverted and now the waters tumble through Kisdon Force behind the hill, and past Keld. Limestone cliffs fringe the hill and Hooker Mill Scar on the western slopes was caused by a huge, ancient landslide. Kisdon Pasture was enclosed in 1832 and cattle once grazed on the bracken where the stone walls shoot up the hillside.

The old Corpse Road passes over the slopes, and close to Kisdon Force the Coast-to-Coast walk crosses the Pennine Way, a favourite route for long-distance walkers. For the less energetic, a walk around the curves of the island hill will be rewarded by marvellous views of Swaledale and the surrounding moors.

Sleddale Head
FROM KIDHOW

This view from limestone pavements on Kidhow is of Sleddale, one of the lovely side dales of Wensleydale. Its stream, Duerly Beck, begins its descent from Oughtershaw and through the dale to Hawes, passing through Gayle. This village was probably built on the site of a Celtic settlement and at one time was larger and more important than Hawes. It is certainly much older, with a warren of narrow alleyways, and a pleasing old three-storey mill beside the beck. This was built in 1784 as a cotton mill, later turning to wool, and it is still in use as a joiner's shop.

Just above the bridge at Gayle there are some particularly attractive waterfalls spilling over the limestone ledges, and further up the valley can be found Aisgill Force, a 30-feet high cataract.

Here, is peace and solitude. The hills roll up on either side, and cattle graze all along the valley, sloping down into the distance and Hawes. The only sounds are of the hurrying water and the curlews which haunt this peaceful scene.

Lady Hill
WENSLEYDALE

Rising clear from the flat floor of Wensleydale, Lady Hill, with its small cluster of trees, is silhouetted gloriously by the sunset. This mound was left by a retreating glacier and where the surrounding, modern farmland meets the rising slopes of the hillsides, evidence of a more ancient method of farming is thrown into relief by the lengthening shadows.

These are the easily recognised, long grassy ridges of the strip lynchets which can be seen in many of the dales. They were made in medieval times and their position on sometimes steep hillsides are an indication of the desperate need of the peasants to grow subsistence crops. Each family in a particular village would be allocated up to five of these strips of land, each being about a furlong long. The medieval ploughs dug a deep 'ridge and furrow' pattern, turning the soil completely over, working from alternate directions. This created the still sharp ridges which follow the contours of the hillside, tapering at each end.

The methods of farming here have left the lynchets undisturbed, and today's farmers are encouraged not to disturb them, so these 'flights' will be preserved as an evocative reminder of the hardship of life here so long ago.

Pendragon Castle
NEAR MALLERSTANG EDGE

Silhouetted against the sky, the few remains of Pendragon Castle on the ridge above Mallerstang, have an alluring mystery about them, enhanced by its supposed connections with King Arthur. His father, Uther Pendragon, is said to have built a castle here. Disappointingly however, the earliest remains do not originate so far back into the mists of time, but have their origins in the 12th century.

Built as a Peel tower by the Normans, it had a commanding view down the valley. It was constructed of wood, and the troublesome Scots invaders made short work of burning it down in 1541; later it came into the hands of the Cliffords of Skipton Castle. 100 years later Lady Anne rebuilt it as an 60-feet square building with three floors. Unfortunately, soon after completion, stones were pilfered, and it was in ruins again within 25 years. Today however, Pendragon Castle is being restored and excavations are revealing more of its structure.

Quaker Meeting House
BRIGFLATTS NEAR SEDBERGH

When the streets of Sedbergh were widened in 1897, the top of the old market cross was removed to nearby Brigflatts, a former flax weavers' hamlet. Here it still stands in the idyllic setting of the garden of the Quaker Meeting House, which it shares with the remnants of an ancient yew tree, under which George Fox preached.

George Fox founded the Quakers, or Society of Friends, in the 1640s. Rejecting the ministry of the established church they suffered violent persecution, but the Anglican church had troubled itself little with this remote area, and when George Fox came to the north in 1652, crowds in excess of 1,000 would gather to hear him speak. There is an inscription marking a rock on Firbank Fell, where he once spoke with such passion and fervour that he gripped the attention of a vast crowd for three hours.

Now, the meeting house, with its mullioned windows and simple furnishings is a haven of peace, and a place of pilgrimage for the Quakers of today.

The Yorkshire Dales Past & Present

This ancient map of the Yorkshire Dales was drawn up in the late sixteenth century by Christopher Saxton (*c.* 1542–*c.* 1610), who became known as 'the Father of English Cartography'. It was just one in a series of 35 maps drawn up by Saxton, covering all the counties of England and Wales. He managed this impressive feat in just five years, between 1574 and 1579.

All 35 maps were bound together and presented in an atlas (issued in 1579) – the first such work to be published in Britain. Saxton's maps remained the definitive guide to the British Isles for several decades; they were also reprinted in 1645 when concise maps were needed during the Civil War. Today this particular map is in the possession of the Royal Geographical Society in London.

Airedale & Malhamdale
27, 31, 81, 93, 98, 152, 187

Dent & Garsdale
21, 25, 35, 37, 100, 116, 124, 133
140, 142, 145, 157, 161, 163, 172, 183, 186

Nidderdale & the East
22, 46, 53, 78, 82, 88, 121, 138, 154, 170, 177, 189

Ribblesdale & the South West
20, 26, 32, 51, 60, 63, 64, 87, 91, 92, 94, 95
97, 101 113, 118, 126, 128, 137, 141, 146, 159, 164, 165, 184

Swaledale & the North West
14, 34, 40, 45, 47, 59, 66, 68, 72, 77, 79, 80, 86, 96, 112
125, 129, 134, 135, 136, 148, 149, 156, 166, 171, 176, 178, 180, 182, 188, 190, 193

Wensleydale
15, 23, 24, 30, 42, 44, 48, 56, 57, 62, 65, 69, 73, 106, 107, 108
109, 115, 117, 120, 130, 131, 132, 139, 144, 158, 160, 162, 173, 179, 191, 192

Wharfedale
16, 18, 19, 36, 38, 39, 41, 50, 52, 58, 74, 76, 90, 104, 105, 114, 147, 153, 174, 181

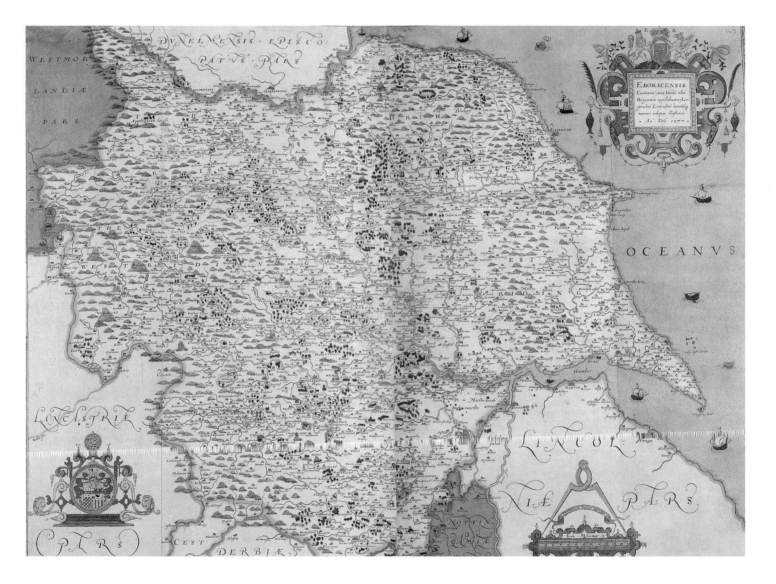

Index